F.A.I.T.H.

Faithful Actions Initiated Through Him

A Twelve Week Discipleship Course For Women

Elizabeth Coker

CROSSBOOKS
PUBLISHING

CrossBooks™
A Division of LifeWay
1663 Liberty Drive
Bloomington, IN 47403
www.crossbooks.com
Phone: 1-866-879-0502

First published by CrossBooks 7/28/2010

ISBN: 978-1-6150-7266-8 (sc)
ISBN: 978-1-6150-7267-5 (hc)

Library of Congress Control Number: 2010909090

Printed in the United States of America
Bloomington, Indiana

This book is printed on acid-free paper.

All scripture referenced in this book is taken from the King James Version of the Holy Bible

DEDICATION

Faith is the greatest legacy I will leave to my children.

This book is dedicated to those special "gifts"
placed in my life from the Lord.

For Dusty, Matthew, Tiffany, Loukas, and Matthew Riley

Contents

ACKNOWLEDGEMENTS

Jesus is the source of my strength and inspiration for all work done to bring glory to Him. This study was inspired by Him. My faith walk is credited to His holding my hand, and to His directing the steps of my life to people who prayed for me and with me. He has blessed me and allowed me to sit under anointed preachers and teachers of His Word. I would wish to honor those local pastors who year after year have preached the Word to their small congregations, especially my pastors. Because they preached, because saints prayed, because evangelists and missionaries left their homes, because of encouragement and edifying through a body of believers, I am walking with the Lord. Thank you to everyone who has been called and answered the call. You are faithful. You are our example of how to become true disciples of the Lord Jesus Christ. I would also like to thank all of the staff of Crossbooks for their gracious help and kind patience in helping to produce this book.

In early 2009 I began to feel that the Lord would have me learn more about how to institute a women's ministry at my local church. I ordered an excellent book that had so many fantastic ideas for getting women started in outreach work, and while I knew the Lord wanted my church to be able to minister in all of the areas described, I realized that most of the women in our small church were fairly new Christians struggling with many trials and were women needing to grow as Christians first before they would be equipped to be introduced to some of the ministry ideals that were in that book. I felt that the Lord then lay on my heart an outline for a series of Bible studies that would equip and inspire women to move quickly through a program of discipleship, a program of discipleship that would take them from an internal focus of their struggles to a God focus of helping others, a program of discipleship that would help to get Christian women off the pews and out into the field to do outreach ministries.

The Lord tells us to put on the whole armor of God so that we will be able to stand against the enemy. Sending ill-equipped soldiers into the harvest is not His best plan for us. A new Christian is equipped to share his testimony as soon as he/she is brought into the kingdom, but it takes some discipleship time to learn the Word and to learn how to battle in the Spirit. Disciples must be taught kingdom principles if they are going to know how to face their giants and defeat them. Too many times we are leaving our new converts wandering through the wilderness trying to figure out their faith walk on their own. *F.A.I.T.H.* was inspired and written to disciple, to encourage, and to challenge women to grow up quickly in the faith so they can get out into the harvest and do the outreach ministries the Lord has designed particularly for women. It is written for my Christian sisters in every denomination, and some of what is taught in these lessons may not be taught in your churches, but it is scriptural and God-inspired to give you the *knowledge* and *power* to do the call God is placing on your life. I ask that you study prayerfully and stay open to the Lord's guidance throughout this study. I believe you will be amazed at what the Lord has planned for your life. My prayers have covered this study and every individual that reads it, and I believe the Lord's anointing is on it. The Lord bless you, precious sisters in Christ.

> **"And Jesus answering saith unto them, Have faith in God." Mark 11:22**

WEEK ONE

Overcoming Fear and Negativity

Welcome to the first in a series of Bible studies I have entitled "F.A.I.T.H. (Faithful Actions Initiated Through Him)." It is my belief that this series of teachings for women will be a catalyst to move you out of your comfort zones, will help you to detect hindrances that are keeping you from being a part of the labor force for the Lord in this last and final harvest, and will help you identify the ministry the Lord is calling you out to do. Effective harvesters know what they are doing and keep laboring until the field is harvested. I believe we all want to be included in that labor force, but we need to overcome some hindrances, gain some knowledge, and understand how to use that knowledge to get there. If you work through these Bible studies and apply them (work the challenges) you will grow, you will overcome, and you will be used effectively of the Lord. I want to tackle two hindrances this first week: negativity and fear.

Do you feel as I do that we are in the last days and that it is harvest time? If you do, you understand how important it is to remove the barriers that are keeping you from being productive in the kingdom and gain the power needed to overcome and help others to be saved. I believe one hindrance to our being productive handmaidens of the Lord is negativity in our talk produced by fear. Fear is in direct opposition to faith. The Word of God says that in the last days men's hearts will fail them for fear. When people go to the doctor, they generally hear that they need to deal with the stress in their life. It is causing high blood pressure or heart problems. That stress is fear. Is there going to be enough work, enough money, enough health, enough time for family? We have so many worries and fears that the Lord wants us to bring to Him. Just rest in Him! Two weeks before I wrote this lesson a tongues and interpretation went forth at an apostolic church in my hometown.

A simple message from the Lord: **"I see your worries and concerns. Come unto me and I will give you rest."** Two weeks later at a church I attended in another town, there was also a tongues and interpretation that basically said, **"Come unto me and I will give you rest. There is nothing too hard for me."** There was more, but my point is that God is the same God, speaking the same thing to His church. He wants us to abide in Him and trust Him. If we abide in the Lord, there is no need for worry or fear. If I could give you a purpose for this teaching today, it is to move us out of "fear" into "faith." The motivation for this would be so we can begin to reach the lost in a greater force than ever before. That is what Jesus commissioned his disciples to do, and if you are following Jesus, you are a disciple. "Fear not!" is said to be in the Bible 366 times, once for every day of the year with even an allowance for leap year.

> "I see your worries and concerns. Come
> unto me and I will give you rest."

Why would God so want us to hear "Fear not?" Because God wants us to trust that He is bigger than our fears? Because He knows that fear will hinder us from doing anything about our purpose? Because God knows we will never do the things we were meant to do if Satan is able to keep us under a paralyzing umbrella of fear? It is all of these and much more, isn't it? I don't know how many of you are feeling this, but it is about to get turned up seven times hotter. Satan is attacking, and those of us remaining cold and lukewarm in the Lord are going to lose more ground than ever. God has called us to be passionate, on fire, and full of zeal for the things of God. **"For God hath not given us the spirit of fear, but of power, and of love, and of a sound mind." (II Timothy 1:7)**

I would like to recall some examples from the Word to help motivate us to turn from fearful living to faithful living. This series of lessons will always focus on women of faith at some point in the lesson. We learn a lot from studying the women of the Bible and how they handled situations. Pay careful attention to what is found praise worthy in these women of faith, and begin to copy those things to become women of faith who get what they ask for, and to become women who win souls for Christ. We can never mobilize ourselves to do what the Lord is calling us to do until we deal with the fear factor and the negativity that operates in our lives. I believe we are all women coming together today who wish to be able to ACT on our FAITH to BEGIN to see more accomplished in our churches, families, schools, and workplaces for the kingdom of God. Revival is coming to those who are hungry for it. If you are ready for the Lord to bring a real hunger for revival and a real thirst for the things of God; if you wish to be a part of the labor force bringing in the end time harvest, pray this prayer aloud asking the Lord to increase all of our faith.

> **Pray this aloud: Father, we acknowledge that you are God and that all power over everything is in the redemptive name of Jesus Christ. We belong to Jesus now and as we abide in Him and He abides in us we know that we can ask anything believing and it shall be done. When we feel fear trying to take hold of us and trying to intimidate us from doing what you have called us to do, help us to turn to you in prayer, whispering your name, until the calm secret place of abiding prevails in us. Whatever we may or may not feel does not cancel out your presence and what you are doing in our lives. Our confidence is in your Word. You promised never to leave us or forsake us. Help us to be filled with your Spirit and the boldness and confidence that it brings to us as we go about as witnesses of the hope that is in you. Increase our faith as we grow in the knowledge of your Word, and take the negativity from our thinking and our tongues. Help us to begin to speak faith more and more each day, speaking it and believing it. Use us as witnesses, Lord. In Jesus name. Amen.**

Turn in your Bibles to Hebrews 11:6. As we examine and discuss scriptures, make use of your handouts at the end of each chapter to write notes, and challenge yourself to memorize the scriptures at the end of the handout every week to help build your faith. Memorizing these scriptures will help you confess positive, rather than negative things into your lives. Take up the challenge at the end of the handout each week to put actions to your faith that you perhaps have not been taking. I will give you a challenge every week, and I believe if you will commit to do those challenges, you will see yourself growing in the things of the Lord, and you will win souls to the Lord.

> "And without faith it is impossible to please God, because anyone who comes to him must believe that he exists and that he rewards those who earnestly seek him." (Hebrews 11:6)

Faith is the opposite of fear. Fear limits God. Faith propels Him. Faith accesses the spiritual realm. Jesus responds to faith. In the book of Mark the disciples may have been limited because of lack of faith on their part, or lack of faith on the part of the father of the boy from whom they were trying to cast out a demon. Anyway, they failed to cast him out. Jesus said, "Oh, faithless generation." The father of the boy said, "I believe, help thou my unbelief." (Mark 9:17-29) It sounds like a contradiction in terms, but today Jesus is saying to many of us, "Oh, faithless generation," and we are saying "I believe, help my unbelief." Everyone can think of a friend or family member right now who needs a healing or deliverance in their lives. I believe that God is showing us in His Word that He means for each of us to be able to pray the prayer of faith to see those things come to pass. We need God's Word. **"So then faith cometh by hearing, and hearing by the word of God." (Romans 10:17)** When you are listening to the Word of God being taught, your faith must increase by the hearing of it. That is how it works and why it is so important to hear preaching and teaching by those anointed of God. Jesus stated that some things would not come out except by prayer and fasting. If we wish to have more power and be effective in our prayers, we will need to live a disciplined and fasted life. That was the final thing that Jesus said to this situation. **"...this kind can by no other means come forth, but by prayer and fasting." (Mark 9:29)** Some things only come out by prayer and fasting. Why? Because prayer and fasting increases our spiritual power and our faith.

It is interesting to note that Jesus had given the disciples power to cast out demons and heal the sick, but they failed to be able to do so. Unbelief can stop the power of God. Faith unleashes the power of God. Even Jesus was unable to do all that he wanted to do in his hometown because of their unbelief. So, we must believe, but the person we are praying for must believe, too, to make the appropriate faith connection to unleash the power needed for the healing or miracle. I believe that all believers would like to be praying for others and seeing the fruit of those prayers manifest. I believe we need some instruction in how faith works, how to pray, and how to hold on to faith when we do not see the immediate manifestation. We also have to begin to step out in faith and **BEGIN** to **DO**. That is **FAITH.**

The Word of God says that we have all been given a measure of faith, so what we need today is to (1)ACT on the faith, (2)SPEAK the Word to the problem, and (3) HELP people stir up faith in them before we pray for them. We need to determine a person's level of belief to be healed before we pray for their healing.

> "Women of Faith, ACT on FAITH, SPEAK the WORD to the problem, and STIR up FAITH BEFORE we pray with people."

Let us consider what may hinder the power that has been given to us. Remember that Jesus gave the disciples power to heal and cast out demons, yet they failed to cast out the demon of a little boy. Unbelief held the power back (the father's lack of faith possibly affected the disciples faith), just as unbelief (that of the people) held Jesus back in his hometown from doing many great miracles. When you received the Holy Ghost, you received power to lay hands on the sick and have them recover, power to lay hands on new believers and see them filled with the Holy Ghost, power to take authority over demons and see them cast out, power to become a bold witness for Christ, no matter in what circumstance you might find yourself. The Word of God says that we receive that power, but many of us are not operating in that power BECAUSE WE ARE NOT OPERATING THAT POWER. The Word of God speaks of those with a **"form of godliness, but lacking the power thereof." (II Timothy 3:5).** So many Christians are afraid of the power, and as long as they are <u>afraid</u> will not walk in the fullness of what God intended for them to walk as His disciples.

This may be a redundant analogy; I have heard it more than a few times, but I still believe it to be effective in illustrating how we have so much power inside of us that we are simply not tapping. The electric outlets in your living room have a great power source available just inside of them.

We cannot see that demonstrated until we tap into them, but it is resident and waiting to be tapped. When I saw my grandson, Loukas, about to stick a nail in an outlet one day, I screamed so loudly at him, that I am sure I scared some years off of his life. Why? Because I know that there is enough power there when tapped into to kill a child or severely hurt him. I did not want my grandson hurt. That power is a good thing when used to give us light, however, isn't it? When we can plug into an outlet and have extended time to do things because it powers artificial light, it helps us.

Jesus said, **"But ye shall receive power, after that the Holy Ghost is come upon you: and ye shall be witnesses unto me both in Jerusalem, and in all Judaea, and in Samaria, and unto the uttermost part of the earth. (Acts 1:8)** Okay, you received the Holy Ghost, and now you have power. What are you doing with the power? Mmhh? What are you doing with the power?

Note this with me, please. The power doesn't operate us; we operate the power. When we are filled with the Holy Ghost, we receive power, but we are the ones who call on and utilize that power. Someone we meet in our daily walk may have a need; the Holy Ghost may help us discern that need, but we make a decision to follow through and use that power to be a bold witness. We allow the Spirit to speak through us when we are praying in the spirit, yes? But if someone interrupts us when we are praying, we can stop praying in the spirit, yes? God is not making us pray; we decide to pray and we allow the Holy Ghost to pray through us. If you are seeking the Holy Ghost at this time, it might help to consider that. God has already made the gift available; allow Him to give it to you. Yield completely to God and receive His gift. (Note: If you have not received the baptism of the Holy Ghost, don't even know you can have it, or if your church does not teach this, I ask you to go through every one of these studies. I will teach you in lesson five from the scriptures what you should be receiving. Please stay with me). In **Proverbs 16:1** it says, **"The preparations of the heart belong to man, but the answer of the tongue is from the Lord."** I love that scripture. We do our part in keeping our heart prepared, submissive, and obedient, and the Lord will have the answer for our tongue in every situation. This is also how to receive the Holy Ghost. It requires an obedient heart. Prepare your heart, purify your heart, obey God, and trust Him. As you do, He will gladly baptize you with His Spirit. If you have received the Holy Ghost, but have never really gotten to a place of "praying in the Spirit," begin to spend time alone with God and ask Him to help you pray in the spirit. If you do not give time to it after you are through praying with the understanding, you are not yielding yourself to the Holy Ghost to allow Him to pray through you some very important things, things that will increase your strength and will intercede in matters for others that you know nothing about. This is more important than you may know, and we are actually commanded to "pray in the Spirit." We all will have times that we approach prayer not even knowing how to begin, not feeling like we can even get started praying, almost feeling like it would be a sin to even start approaching God with how down or lifeless we feel about praying right then. Know that God will help us pray. Follow these steps when you feel that way. (1)Sing a song of praise first. (2)Then begin to praise and thank Him for everything you can remember that He has done for you. (He inhabits the praise of His people and truly this praise and thanksgiving is how we should always go into His courtyard, inviting His presence.) (3)From this point you will be able to settle into real communion with God and begin to intercede for others and supplicate for your needs. Your prayer life will only grow as your faith grows, and vice versa, so it is important to move from shallow prayer to deeper prayer, if you wish to move from shallow faith to deeper faith.

> "It is important to move from shallow prayer to deeper prayer, if you wish to move from shallow faith to deeper faith."

Woman of Faith
The Shunammite Woman

Who got results in the Bible? Our first week's woman of faith is the Shunnamite woman. This scripture reading may seem lengthy, but it is important to get the complete story to understand the level of this woman's faith.

> And it fell on a day, that Elisha passed to Shunem, where was a great woman; and constrained him to eat bread. And so it was, that as oft as he passed by, he turned in thither to eat bread. And she said unto her husband, Behold now, I perceive that this is an holy man of God, which passeth by us continually. Let us make a little chamber, I pray thee, on

the wall; and let us set for him there a bed, and a table, and a stool, and a candlestick: and it shall be, when he cometh to us, that he shall turn in thither. And it fell on a day, that he came thither, and he turned into the chamber, and lay there. And he said to Gehazi his servant, Call this Shunammite. And when he had called her, she stood before him. And he said unto him, Say now unto her, Behold, thou hast been careful for us with all this care; what is to be done for thee? Wouldest thou be spoken for to the king, or to the captain of the host? And she answered, I dwell among mine own people. And he said, What then is to be done for her? And Gehazi answered, Verily she hath no child, and her husband is old. And he said, Call her. And when he had called her, she stood in the door. And he said, About this season, according to the time of life, thou shalt embrace a son. And she said, Nay, my lord, thou man of God, do not lie unto thine handmaid. And the woman conceived, and bare a son at that season that Elisha had said unto her, according to the time of life. And when the child was grown, it fell on a day, that he went out to his father to the reapers. And he said unto his father, My head, my head. And he said to a lad, Carry him to his mother. And when he had taken him, and brought him to his mother, he sat on her knees till noon, and then died. And she went up, and laid him on the bed of the man of God, and shut the door upon him, and went out. And she called unto her husband, and said, Send me, I pray thee, one of the young men, and one of the asses, that I may run to the man of God, and come again. And he said, Wherefore wilt thou go to him today? It is neither new moon, nor Sabbath. And she said, It shall be well. Then she saddled an ass, and said to her servant, Drive, and go forward; slack not thy riding for me, except I bid thee. So she went and came unto the man of God to mount Carmel. And it came to pass, when the man of God saw her afar off, that he said to Gehazi his servant, Behold, yonder Is that Shunammite: Run now, I pray thee, to meet her, and say unto her, Is it well with thee? Is it well with thy husband? Is it well with the child? And she answered, It is well. And when she came to the man of God to the hill, she caught him by the feet: but Gehazi came near to thrust her away. And the man of God said, Let her alone; for her soul is vexed within her: and the LORD hath hid it from me, and hath not told me. Then she said, Did I desire a son of my lord? Did I not say, Do not deceive me? Then he said to Gehazi, Gird up thy loins, and take my staff in thine hand, and go thy way: if thou meet any man, salute him not; and if any salute thee, answer him not again: and lay my staff upon the face of the child. And the mother of the child said, As the Lord liveth, and as thy soul liveth, I will not leave thee. And he arose, and followed her. And Gehazi passed on before them, and laid the staff upon the face of the child; but there was neither voice, nor hearing. Wherefore he went again to meet him, and told him, saying, The child is not awaked. And when Elisha was come into the house, behold, the child was dead, and laid upon his bed. He went in therefore, and shut the door upon them twain, and prayed unto the Lord. And he went up, and lay upon the child, and put his mouth upon his mouth, and his eyes upon his eyes, and his hands upon his hands: and he stretched himself upon the child; and the flesh of the child waxed warm. Then he returned, and walked in the house to and fro; and went up, and stretched himself upon him: and the child sneezed seven times, and the child opened his eyes. And he called Gehazi, and said, Call this Shunammite. So he called her. And when she was come in unto him, he said, Take up thy son. Then she went in, and fell at his feet, and bowed herself to the ground, and took up her son, and went out. (II Kings 4:8-37)

The Shunammite woman got results. Let us break down what makes this woman a great woman of faith, something I believe you very much want to be or you would not be bothering to read this study. The Shunammite woman is called a great woman in the Old Testament scriptures. She extends herself to the prophet Elisha every time he comes by her way; he knows he is welcome to stop and eat with her. She has asked her husband to allow a room for him that he may turn in and stay and rest when he is in their area. She is kind, and she understands the principle of giving her carnal things to repay the minister for his spiritual things he is imparting. When we become givers and lovers of others, we will begin to allow the power of God to operate through us more. Find a way to give all of the time. Not just money, but time, love, and care. The Shunammite woman got the attention of the prophet through her faithfulness to meet his needs. This faithfulness gets his attention, just like our faithfulness gets God's attention. If you want to see God's hand in your daily life, start being faithful in study of His Word, in praying daily to Him, in church attendance, in tithes, offerings, and every good work that presents itself to you, and as you lead that consecrated life, blessings and miracles will follow. What follows the Shunammite woman's good works to the prophet is that he finds out she is without child and her husband is old. He tells her she will have a child. She is afraid to hope for what she has hoped for and says, "No" in disbelief. Have you ever been there? Afraid to hope for what you hope for, because not getting it is too big of a disappointment to handle? She does have a son, and there is a day when he dies in her lap. She tells her husband and later Gehazi that "All is well." She goes and lays her boy on the prophet's bed that is in her house.

SHE DOES NOT SPEAK ONE NEGATIVE THING!

She does not even tell her husband the boy has died. How many of you know that other people can sabotage our faith? Sometimes, we have to stay very quiet before others about what we believe God has spoken to us. I have a few people that I cannot speak about what God is doing in my life, because they are naysayers, and my faith wilts a bit around them. It is important whom you surround yourself with, isn't it? You can be happy as a lark, and someone comes around speaking the negative and you feel your spirit becoming cast down with them. We need to be encouraging others, but the Word of God tells us to also encourage ourselves in spiritual hymns and psalms, so even if you are not singing artist of the world, you need to sing to encourage yourself. Sing praises to God. It works. There is a song that says, "He lifts me up in spirit when I lift Him up in praise; it seems the more I praise the Lord the happier my days. By lifting Jesus higher, the less my burden weighs, He lifts me up in spirit when I lift Him up in praise." It works. Stay positive: Sing. You may believe for a healing from God, but others will try to get you to the doctor. Hold on to your faith quietly sometimes.

The Shunammite woman is well aware that her son has died, but she has established a relationship with a prophet of God in her past, and FAITH kicks in. She saddles a donkey and rides to get the prophet, after laying her son on the prophet's bed at her house. She does not accept a substitute to go to her house (the servant Gehazi), but she insists that she will not leave until the prophet comes. She goes across protocol in approaching Elisha in this way, but her service to him makes her demands acceptable. Earlier in her relationship with Elisha she will not go beyond standing in his door. Now, desperation takes her past protocol and she is bowing before him holding his feet, demanding of him. Have you ever reached a point of demanding of God? If you do not have a relationship, you do not have the right. A few times I have said firmly to God, "You have to do something." No, I do not order God around, and I reverence Him at all times, but I have a relationship with my daddy, and when there is a need and I am at the end of my ability, I can demand, and He takes care of it because He knows I am doing my part; I serve Him; I am consecrated to Him; I have a relationship with Him. Do you have a circumstance like the Shunammite woman, where someone or something SEEMS dead? Maybe you feel your son or daughter is dead in sin; just put them on the altar of God and confess "All is well." Let your faith save your household. Develop your relationship with God, and have confidence to go to Him with all of your needs the same way that the Shunammite woman had confidence to go to Elisha for help because she had already served him. God will more quickly attend to us if we are keeping his attention through service and relationship. The Shunammite woman's son lived again. She got results through service, relationship, and speaking the right thing: "All is well." I wish that you would think of some problem right now that keeps tying you up in knots. Do you have a picture of that problem? Say aloud, "All is well." Say it again, please. "All is well."

Really, God has it under control. Give it to him. This was a great woman of faith whom we should all emulate through extending kindnesses to all, but particularly those who are our ministering pastors and evangelists, those of the household of faith, not to get a return; however, God does bless those who are obedient and faithful.

Fear would speak negativity. "My son is dead." "He has been dead for a long time." "I don't know how he can be saved." "I am broke." "I am depressed." "I am lonely." "I am without help." "I cannot make it." I want to pause just a moment here and allow you to think of something negative you have been confessing. Write it down in your notes at the end of this chapter. Let's see if we can turn that negative statement into a positive confession of faith.

Faith would speak positively: "My son is well." "He is coming home." "I trust God--He is bringing my kids in." "God will provide." "God is my Comforter and my friend." "God is a very present help in time of need." "I can do all things through Christ which strengtheneth me." "He is able to do abundantly above all that I can ask or think according to the power that works in us." Have you ever examined this oft quoted scripture? It doesn't say He does abundantly above because of the power *that is in Him*, but He does it because of the *power that works in us. Not the power that exists in us, but the power that works in us. How does this power work in us?*

His Spirit+His Word+Our Faith+Our Confession+ACTION

Do something for me. Take a slip of paper and a pen. I want you to write the name of someone on that paper. The name you will write is the name of someone you love who you are so focused on all of the time, worrying whether they will be saved. I want you to fold that paper with that name and lay it on your home altar. God has work for you to do. He is going to take care of that person. He wants you to give Him that burden, and He wants you to take up your cross to help those around you get to their altar.

The Shunammite woman is an Old Testament example of a very special woman of faith. In the New Testament, Jesus relays a parable of a woman who keeps going before an unjust judge. He finally answers her request just because he knows that she is not going to give up, just like the Shunammite woman. She is going to weary him until she gets what she wants. He gives her what she asks for as well. We get answers to our prayers when we have been faithful in service and communion, but I also see Jesus responding to the desperate and the persistent. Scripture says that **"The effectual, fervent prayer of a righteous man availeth much." (James 5:16)** Don't give up ever. That is right when the breakthrough is about to happen--when some have quit.

In Mark 7:24-30, it is related that a Syrophoenician woman approaches Jesus, asking for her daughter to be healed of a wrong spirit. Jesus answers, "Is it meet to give the children's bread to the dogs?" She is well aware of the racist way the Jews refer to the Gentiles, and dismisses this without offense, and says, "Even the dogs eat from the children's table." She is not offended and her faith is not dampened. If we get offended at the Word of God or at other people, our spirit will not be right for faith to operate. We are not to get offended, period. Shake off the hurt, the misunderstandings, and pray for those who do you wrong. Let it go immediately. We do not have time for offense. There is too much kingdom work to do, and we do not want to hinder that work. A lot of people think that Jesus was referencing women as dogs, and was being very insulting to her. Does that really sound like Jesus? I do not even think that this was a woman thing, but he was really stating what the Jews felt toward all Gentiles, male or female. How something is said changes the meaning oftentimes, and I doubt that Jesus spoke harshly to this woman. I can almost see him looking intently with interest at this woman as she pleads for his help with her daughter, and perhaps baiting her with what she already knows she is known as with the Jewish people, waiting to see what she will do or say, how she will respond. She answers in a way that is submissive to whatever category he wishes to place her in--only heal her child. Her faith, as well as her humility, is obvious. We do not receive anything when we are in pride. The door is closing to the Jews here that don't want what Jesus if offering and opening to the Gentiles--you and me--the ones who get grafted in to the promises of Abraham that were meant for the Jews--we become a royal priesthood and children of the king following Calvary. I think this moment and the woman's response is so important to realize how connected our attitudes are to operate faith. Submission, obedience, and humility to the order of God and to His Word is so important to the operation of our faith. Whatever you say, Lord. Just obey what He is going to start asking you to do when you decide to fully submit to Him. We need to empty ourselves out, so there is only room for God in our vessel and His purpose for our lives.

> "If we get offended at the Word of God or at other people,
> our spirit will not be right for faith to operate."

Here is the faith connection I see with the three women I have mentioned. The Shunammite woman is consecrated, faithful, takes care of the prophet's needs (today that would mean faithful in tithes, offerings, and service to the church), and she holds onto faith in God even when the circumstance says, "Too late!" She is not too proud to go across protocol to get what she wants from God. She refuses to speak the negative, even though the circumstance is negative. The Syrophoenician woman believes Jesus can cast out demons; she believes He will extend Himself beyond the children of Israel because of her faith; she is determined to get what she needs even if she has to humble herself to insults to get it.

The woman going before the unjust judge understands what is right and is determined to have what is coming to her. If we press through asking for what we see in the Word of God is ours to receive, certainly a just God would provide what we are asking for, if an unjust judge would give it just to have us shut up and leave him alone. God is pleased when we ask, when we seek, when we believe. Remember that He told the disciples to tarry until they received power. We are disciples too. Tarry and keep knocking. He wants to answer. Keep knocking! Keep confessing your faith! These women have FAITH!!! They are not turned aside to look for their healing somewhere else because of resistance of the ones that they are asking for help. We should not turn aside from helping people to come to God and get what they need because they are resistant to receive our word or God's Word. We should keep going "again" to get them to God, and to get what we need from God, we should keep seeking until we obtain. Don't stop believing when you do not see an immediate response. Faith never quits.

Again, Faith is the opposite of Fear!

We are supposed to be walking by faith. We are to believe supernaturally for the existence of something we cannot see with the natural eye. How do we walk in faith? We know what the Word of God says. We speak the Word of God to any adverse circumstance that presents itself in our lives. We abide in God and allow Him to abide in us, and then we know that we can ask anything and He will see that it is done. We obey the Word, and as we do we will have a confidence to go before the throne of God, and we will increase our faith every time we see another answer come from God. If exercising muscle builds muscle, know that exercising faith builds faith. We openly confess our belief in the power of our master. We do not negate that belief through negative confession. Just be quiet if it is negative. Speak it aloud if it is a positive confession in your healing and God's power to heal. **"Faith is the substance of things hoped for, the evidence of things not seen." (Hebrews 11:1)** Do not negate what God wants you to have in your life and what he wants to use you to do to help save the lost by opening your mouth and saying the wrong thing; do not have a wrong attitude toward God or the ministry that he sets over you. When you don't know what to say or what to do, or you are lacking courage to do what you know to do, try this: **"Wait on the Lord: be of good courage, and he shall strengthen thine heart: wait, I say, on the Lord." (Psalm 27:14)**

The Shunammite woman had courage and she knew how to wait. The circumstance said that her son died in her lap. Her action is not to begin wailing, but to send for a ride to get to the prophet. Why will the prophet of God consider her appeal, and even more, send someone out to meet her when he sees her coming? She has aided him in the past. She has provided for his needs. They have a relationship. She has served him, so she has a right to ask him to meet her needs. She goes directly to the prophet with her need in this Old Testament dispensation, but we go directly to God with our needs in this New Testament dispensation of grace. God wants to have relationship with us; he wants to save us, deliver us, heal us, comfort us, but relationship requires our obedience, our faithfulness, our service to Him. Helping others get to God and interceding for their needs requires our relationship with God. The word "wait" can mean several things, can't it? If you are a waitress, it means to "serve;" if you do not get in any hurry, if you can have patience and just "hold on," then you understand how to "wait" on the Lord. His timing is rarely our timing, and His ways are not our ways. Trust God! Have faith!

"If you abide in Me, and my words abide in you, ask what you will, it shall be done unto you." (John 15:4) Some of us are disappointed when we ask God to do something for us, and we are not seeing anything happen. Are you abiding in Him, in the study of His Word, in speaking His word, in conversation, praise, thanksgiving, and supplication prayer? It is a covenant relationship, a contract, not a one-sided, God-do-it-all relationship. He requires our obedience to show that we love him, and then we are allowed to access His favor and blessings.

If you are operating in the negative, you are under stress which equals fear. Jesus said that men's hearts would fail them for fear in the last days. Well…? So many people are going to the doctor with heart problems. The doctor tells them they must deal with stress. What is stress? It is fear, isn't it?

What is the antidote to fear? It is faith. How do we grow our faith? We act on the measure of faith given to every one of us; we remember that Jesus said, "If you have faith as a grain of mustard, you could speak to this mountain and it would be removed." And we believe what he said. We say and pray as the disciples did to Jesus, "Lord, increase our faith." We get mad at all of the confusion and attacks brought against us by Satan, and we learn to keep that part of our armor up that is called "the shield of faith" and we start fighting back with "the sword of the Spirit" which is the Word of God. To fight back with the Word of God, we must know the Word of God.

Scripture says that we perish for lack of knowledge. How much Word do you know? How much time are you giving to studying the Word? How much Word are you speaking to the problems that come to you and those you love and are praying for? Courage is not the absence of fear; it is the ability to keep moving forward even when you feel the fear. As you face the giants and move forward, the fear will be replaced by faith. You must proceed in your walk of faith. You must take action to become the bold witnesses that God has already given you the power to be. Activate the power! Using a secular example, Eleanor Roosevelt once said, "I believe that anyone can conquer "fear" by doing the things he fears to do, provided he keeps doing them until he gets a record of successful experiences behind him." That takes us back to exercising faith. It gets better the more you practice it. This is a woman who was afraid to speak before others. If she had not overcome that fear, her husband who was hiding out of the public eye, overcome with depression from being stricken by polio, probably would not have ever been able to enter the presidency. She conquered her fear, and kept the Roosevelt name alive, speaking before others and being a forerunner of his campaign. If you are waiting to speak to others until Satan stops telling you how stupid you are going to look, you are going to be waiting a long time. Let me just tackle the "stupid" thing for you. There will always be the unbelieving around to mock you, to talk about you, to think that you do look stupid when you are speaking of the things of God. We are to speak anyway. I really do not care if anyone thinks that I sound stupid or simple. I know that I know that my God has saved me from hell, and I know that I know that if we do not stop worrying about how we are going to look to others, there are going to be many of our family members and neighbors who will go to hell. Is it worth looking stupid to you to save someone's soul? What did God deliver you from?

**Whatever God has delivered you from, is one area where
He desires you to become a forerunner of deliverance!**

What am I saying? If you have been delivered from drugs, you are going to be able to help others get delivered. If you have been delivered from immorality, you are going to be able to help precious young men and women get delivered from immorality. If you have overcome pride and vanity, you can help people in that area. To have the revival God is ready to send, we must pray and intercede for souls, and we must move beyond patty cake prayers to spending some intense prayer meetings daily, calling on God for the revival that He is wanting to send when we get hungry enough. How badly do you want your kids saved, your co-workers saved, your friends at school, and your family saved? How badly do you want to be able to pray with a friend for a healing and see the miracle done?

Ask God right now to help you this week to step out in faith toward a direction he has been leading you in, to witness to a person you have been afraid to go to, to offer to pray for a friend in the world who needs healing or deliverance. Ask Him to help you ACT. Nothing is accomplished through good intentions. Trust Him to give you wisdom and leading.

Look at the worksheet at the end of the chapter. Consider the Syrophoenician woman's submissiveness, and consider how submissive you are to authority in your life and answer the questions you see there. Take a few minutes to consider and write honest responses to the questions. You are the only one who is going to see those answers, unless you choose to share with someone, but we need to examine this part of our lives if we are going to be used by God.

Don't lose sight of the **F.A.I.T.H.** acronym on the worksheet as you work through this Bible study. It stands for **Faithful Actions Initiated Through Him.** This acronym should remind you that **"In Him I live and move and have my being." (Acts 17:28)** If we abide in Him and He abides in us, remember, we can ask what we want and it will be done. **IF!** He requires our obedience. We need to ask him to set up the divine appointments he wants us to have with the people in our lives this week. We need to ask Him for His wisdom in speaking to them. As we live *through* Him and let Him live *through* us, and allow Him to lead us, our faithful actions will become an automatic response to serving Him, and we will be laborers in this final harvest. Your challenge this week is to write down one step of faith that you want the Lord to help you to take to become a soul winner for Him. You already know the thoughts that have been placed in your mind about certain people whom you need to talk to about God. Write down now those names on your worksheet and pray for wisdom and divine appointments with them. If you have been battling fear in an area, I would like for you to pray aloud the prayer on this page. We are living in a fearful world. Even the Old Testament prophets battled fear after some of their greatest victories, so I am sure we all need prayer against the fear, prayer to go forth in courage, trusting God to take care of the fear factor, as we step out in faith. God is bringing revival to the churches that want it, but we are going to have to lose the fear, and step out in faith if we are going to be a part of that revival and harvest of souls.

F.A.I.T.H.

Faithful Actions Initiated Through Him

Pray this aloud: Lord, we know that without you we cannot effectively do anything. We are asking for your wisdom and leadership every day from this point forward to recognize the opportunities to witness, to help us allow you to lead us through those divine appointments. We are asking you to help us eliminate fearfulness from our lives through the knowledge and confession of your Word in every situation that Satan or our own flesh may throw up to us to deter us from doing Your will. We know that the end draws close, Lord, and we are asking You to hold us close to You to empower us for Your service, to imbue us with power from on high that we become the godly bold witnesses that You desire us to be. Help us to take a step of faith each day this week, and help us to spend time in the study of Your Word and on our knees before You before we undertake any service for You. You are a light unto our feet and a lamp unto our path. We await Your guidance and direction and ask that You would give us courage and confidence to begin to obey You immediately in all that You are asking us to do. I am asking that You bless each of us, Lord, with a divine unction in our spirit to follow through on what You have been leading us to do for You. I am asking that You would fill us with the Holy Spirit, because without

the leading of Your Spirit, we will not be effective in this work. I am asking that You would bless us and our families, and as we lay our loved ones on the altar, I am asking that You would give us an assurance that You are taking care of our loved ones, and that we can trust You with that burden, because You need to trust us with the work of the harvest. Help us to place a new trust in You tonight, Lord, and to begin to deny ourselves pleasures of this world that we might present our bodies to You a holy sacrifice for Your service. Bless us indeed, Lord, in our families and in our churches, giving us an enlargement of territory to take back from the enemy. Let us be guided by Your Hand in each step we take each day and in each divine appointment You make for us. Protect us from the evil one. We want to exalt You in the lives that we lead this week, Lord. Help us to do that. I love You, Father. In Jesus Name be glorified. Amen.

This week: Review the worksheets, making notes from the lesson that you wish to remember, memorize the scriptures, and work the challenge that is outlined for you. Also memorize the **F.A.I.T.H.** acronym to hold onto to remind you that you aren't doing anything until you run it by and through the Holy Spirit. Only when you know you have His leading do you proceed to ACT.

WEEK ONE WORKSHEETS

Overcoming Fear and Negativity
With Positive Confession and God's Word

Use your worksheets to respond to the scriptures in the lesson each week and as you meditate on the scriptures and the thoughts brought out in the lesson, make sure to write a note of anything the Lord is speaking to your heart through these lessons, or make a note of any person He may bring to your mind.

Hebrews 11:6 "And without faith it is impossible to please God, because anyone who comes to him must believe that he exists and that he rewards those who earnestly seek him."

Notes:

____

____

____

____

How did we say to plug in to the power?

The Power That Works in Us

His Spirit
+
His Word
+
Our Faith
+
Our Confession
+
Our Action

**"The preparations of the heart belong to man, but
the answer of the tongue is from the Lord."
Proverbs 16:1**

It cannot be stressed enough how important it is that we learn to pray to stay in relationship with the Lord and to keep our hearts right before Him. When we prepare our hearts, He prepares our blessings. Note here anything you remember from the lesson about how to get started praying and get in His presence *when you don't feel like praying.*

Notes

____

____

____

____

We want to be fruitful in our ministry. We want to see souls saved, people healed, and people delivered. Jesus said we should do even greater miracles now. Why? We can do them because the body of Christ continues to grow. There are more hands, more feet, and more mouths to share this gospel, to lay hands on people, and to pray. God is not limiting Himself to one body on earth anymore. We are the body. I hope you get a revelation of how powerful that is. Satan is not just under Jesus feet, as you may think in your mind; He is under our feet, the body of Jesus Christ.

Week One Woman of Faith

The Shunammite Woman
II Kings 4:8-37

Notes:

____

____

____

____

When we speak negatively, we are speaking **FEAR**
(False evidence appearing real)
When we speak positively and act, we are speaking **F.A.I.T.H.**
(Faithful actions initiated through Him).

Do you understand what I mean by this F.A.I.T.H. acronym?

____

____

____

**"He is able to do abundantly above all that I can ask or
think according to the power that works in us."**

He is the power in us, but we must activate that power through faith to see the mighty things of God performed in our lives. Power in our lives must be initiated through Him. We can't bypass Him; we can't do anything without Him. We must have His power working in us and through us and act on what he initiates for us to do for Him.

We must SPEAK our faith to overcome our fears
and to mobilize ourselves out of passivity, out of
our comfort zones, and out of our inertia.

Consider the Syrophoenician Woman
Mark 7:25-30

Note here how you respond to authority:

____

Are you submissive and honoring of your husband?

____

Are you submissive and honoring of your parents?

____

Are you submissive and honoring of your pastors?

____

**If you are going to be used by God, he needs you to
honor all authority He has placed in your life before
you can go forward to lead in any capacity.**

How quickly do you obey God when you feel Him nudging you to do something?

____

Check and release any judgmental attitudes here. We can't have those and minister to anyone's needs.

Are you racist?

____

Are you critical?

____

Are you judgmental?

____

Do you see yourself as more righteous than your sisters in the Lord?

____

Do you talk about your brothers and sisters in the Lord in the negative?

____

Or compare yourself with them?

____

If you feel resistance or conviction in your heart from considering any of the above questions, please pray this next week for God to help you to have the proper respect for all authority, and the proper humility before

God and your brothers and sisters as He uses you in His kingdom work. We must have a right spirit and a teachable spirit.

Make a note here of what you may need to pray and study about concerning authority and humility during this next week. Write questions that come to your mind to prompt further study of the subject of submitting yourself.

____

____

____

How do we grow our faith?

____

____

How do we overcome fear and negativity?

____

____

Scripture Memorization

If you have never practiced memorizing scriptures weekly, I want to strongly challenge you to do this. Write a couple of these scriptures on a note card and carry it with you and set it by where you are working and quote it mentally several times a day and by the end of the week you will have it--a Word with power from the Lord that you have hid in your heart--a Word that you can bring forth someday when you need to encourage yourself in the Lord, or when you are battling in the Spirit. His Word is awesome!

"Now faith is the substance of things hoped for, the evidence of things not seen." Hebrews 11:1

"Wait on the Lord, be of good courage, and he shall strengthen thine heart. Wait, I say, on the Lord." Psalm 27:14

"If you abide in Me, and my words abide in you, ye shall ask what you will, and it shall be done unto you." John 15:7

**"The apostles said to the Lord, 'Increase our
faith!'" Luke 17:5 <u>PRAY THIS DAILY</u>**

**"My people perish for want of knowledge. Since you have rejected
knowledge, I will reject you from my priesthood; Since you have
ignored the Law of your God, I will ignore your sons." Hosea 4:6**

STUDY THE WORD

WE ARE ACCOUNTABLE IF WE REJECT
THE STUDY OF HIS WORD

Write down one step of faith that you want the Lord to help you to take
this week to become a soul winner for Him. Ask Him specifically to give
you wisdom and strength to take that step of faith.

____

____

____

____

____

____

____

____

____

F.A.I.T.H.

Faithful Actions Initiated Through Him

**Allow this acronym to remind you that "In Him I live and move and
have my being." As we live through Him and let Him live through
us, and allow Him to lead us, our faithful actions will become an
automatic response to serving Him and caring about saving others.
Faith without works is dead.**

This Week's Challenge

Do one thing each day this week that moves you out of passivity and your comfort zone. Write down in a journal what you did. As you begin to get reactions to "stepping out in faith," go back and write in the date that you saw fruit from your faith action. Write prayers prayed and dates answered. Jesus said, **"Cast thy bread upon the waters, for thou shalt find it after many days." (Ecclesiastes 11:1)** You will not see immediate results of all of the "seed" that you will "sow," but after many days, the seed and the bread will bring a harvest. We sow, but only God knows how it will end up. Our pleasure is in obeying the command to "GO!" A lot of other faithful people have sown, and we are going to be partakers of their harvest as well.

WEEK TWO

Overcoming Hurt Caused By Others and Ourselves

Week one, we talked about overcoming fear and negativity in our talk that could be hindering us from receiving things by faith when we pray. If we are in fear, we learned, we are not in faith. Our negative talk can hinder us from receiving those things we are trying to believe God for in our lives. In this lesson we are going to do our study concerning overcoming hurt caused by others and ourselves.

> **Pray this aloud: Father, Help us to understand the mercy that you have made available to us. Enlighten us to realize that your mercies are truly new every day, and they are not just to us, but they are to all of those who have hurt us in the past. We receive your mercy and thank you for it, Lord! With your help, I am releasing all hurt to you. In Jesus name. Amen.**

All of my scripture references come from the King James version of the Bible. You may wish to read what I present in the amplified version.

> "That it might be fulfilled that was spoken by Esais, the prophet, saying, Behold my servant, whom I have chosen, my beloved, in whom my soul is well pleased; I will put my spirit upon him, and he will shew judgment to the Gentiles. He shall not strive nor cry, nor shall any man hear his voice in the streets. A bruised reed shall he not break, and smoking flax shall he not quench, till he send forth judgment unto victory. (Matthew 12:17-21)

The Lord did not come to condemn. He came to save. He came to give us victory over sin, not condemnation. If there was much sin in our past, we can sometimes allow condemnation to take hold of us again after our salvation experience, but condemnation never comes from God; it only comes from Satan, others, or ourselves. Jesus did not come to condemn. Some of you have received God's forgiveness, but maybe you are still bowed down in your haunted house, allowing Satan to forever remind you of your past, or you are allowing people to control you with their attitudes about your past. When Jesus said, "It is finished" on the cross of Calvary, our forgiveness and healing were completed. We just have to claim that once and for all and walk in the victory he has already paid the price for on Calvary.

I am writing about overcoming hurt caused by others and ourselves. In **Matthew 12:21**, it is stated **"A bruised reed shall he not break, and smoking flax shall he not quench, till he send forth judgment unto victory."** We need to discover what is actually being said here. A reed would be a plant that would grow in marshy ground. It has a hollow cylinder that is very strong, strong enough to be used as a wind instrument, unless it is bruised. Because of the hollow cylinder of a reed, if it has damage or is bruised, it is too weak to do much good. Most people would break it off and throw it away. Most people want to throw away those of us who have been broken through abuse and sin. Jesus won't throw us away, though. He will not refuse those of us who have been bruised in our lives. What do I mean by bruised? I mean emotional bruising; I mean the hurts we have received that have done damage to our personalities and spirits and self-esteem. I mean the hurts that no one else may know about. Jesus cares about us and about the hurt that others have caused, and he also cares about the self-destructive hurts we have caused ourselves through addictions and sinful choices. He came to heal all of that.

The second part of what we are looking at in that scripture is the "smoking flax." The smoking flax is the wick of an oil lamp, just smoking. A smoking flax does not have any flame, so most people would snuff it on out, but Jesus would send forth "judgment unto victory." The spiritual application here is that those of us who have almost had our flame extinguished due to trials and cares of life, who have almost lost our desire to do the work we should be doing, Jesus is still willing to receive us, to help us fan a flame again into our lives. The backslider He is willing to receive again and to help stir you up into a light He can use to help win others to Him.

There may be some humans who will not have confidence in you for a while because you turned back, but God can see the intents of hearts and He will receive a broken backslider who is ready to repent and start following the Lord again. Those of us who may have grown cold in our spirits He is trying to fan the flame and get us burning bright for Him again. He is not throwing us away. I hope that you also know that you are responsible to stir yourself up, and not let your flame for the things of God to be quenched. The Word of God says that it would be better to be cold than lukewarm. Why? Because someone who is cold hasn't ever known the Lord, but someone who is lukewarm has known the Lord, but isn't loving and appreciating and delighting in the Lord after all He has given to you. I hope that you will help stir yourselves up to be used fully of the Lord, that you will resist feeling like you can't be used because of your past, or because of present circumstances you may be in now. The Lord has a purpose for every life; he had a purpose for you when you were still in your mother's womb. Those of us who know how to stay broken before Him He will receive.

> **"For I know the plans I have for you, declares the
> Lord, plans to prosper you and not to harm you, plans
> to give you a hope and a future. (Jeremiah 29:11)**

How many of you know that nothing is too hard for God? That His arm is not shortened that it cannot save? He can reach to the lowest pit to pull someone up to His salvation. They just need to call out to Him. He pulled some of us out of a very low pit. I think that one of my favorite testimonies I have heard through the years is that of a young man who recounted that when he was a young boy he used to go to the dump and collect broken pieces of colored glass. He would clean them up for his collection. When he was saved, the Lord told him that he was like those broken pieces of glass. God could clean him up, too, so that he would sparkle again. If we will let God, He knows how to take the broken pieces of our lives and put them together again in a new way for his purpose, a better plan than any we have ever had. Trust Him to know what is best for your life and see the masterpiece He can create of your life.

We live in a culture today of broken people, of women who have already done so much damage to themselves before they even hear of the goodness of Jesus. How does Jesus deal with all of the sin in our society today? Has it become too big of a job for Him to handle? Let's look at how Jesus handled things when He walked on earth among us.

> "And straightening up, Jesus says, Woman, where are they? Did no one condemn thee? And she said, No one, Lord. Neither do I condemn you; go your way; From now on sin no more." (John 8: 10-11)

He did not condemn the sinner. He did admonish the sinner to go and sin no more, and I think this is where we may miss it today. We are trying to obtain grace and still remain sinners.

This response of Jesus follows the story of the adulteress being brought to Jesus and thrown down before him, with the Pharisees demanding what should be done to her to test Jesus. Moses had said she should be stoned. (We did notice that the man committing adultery with the woman was not brought before Jesus, yes?) Jesus stooped down and wrote in the sand. He is so kind. He does not want to humiliate any of us, not the adulterous woman, not the men standing there with their own sinful backgrounds. Maybe he is writing some of their sins in the sand. I don't know, but when he says, "Let the one without sin be the first to cast the stone," they begin to leave from the oldest to the youngest.

The sin of adultery is wrong. The sin of fornication is wrong. Jesus says that it is the only sin committed with the flesh. Our bodies are to be the temple of the Holy Ghost, so you understand the depth of this sin if you are living for God. We have come up in this generation to see women's sexuality promoted, and the idea of abstinence before marriage scoffed at by the world. Those of us who weren't raised in church, or did not have a relationship with God during high school and college years no doubt followed the world's ways of dealing with sexuality. We did not learn the value of staying pure for our husband's only. We lost something precious. However, like the adulterous woman in the above story, Jesus is not condemning us. He is saying, "No condemnation--go and sin no more."

If after coming to the Lord in repentance, being baptized in Jesus name for the remission of those sins, and being filled with the baptism of the Holy Ghost, you are still feeling condemnation for those past sins, I can assure you that that condemnation is not coming from God. Satan wants to bring up your past, and there may be some self-righteous brothers and sisters who want to give you the evil eye of judgment, but condemnation is never from God. Conviction of sins comes from the Lord, so that you can correct error, and move away from sin, not so you can walk cowed down like the worst sinner of the world. He wants us to be victorious. It is so important not to allow condemnation to attach itself to us. God's anointing cannot rest on condemnation. This is why Satan so wants to keep you under condemnation. You can't operate in faith if you are in condemnation, so he keeps us chained to do nothing for God, because he has convinced us that we are not worthy. God's Word says:

> **"There is therefore now no condemnation to those who are in Christ Jesus." Therefore, if any man be in Christ, he is a new creature: old things are passed away, ALL things are become new." (II Corinthians 5:17)**

This scripture alone is enough to help us understand the grace of God and the work that Jesus did on Calvary. You are not that old girl anymore. You are no longer a liar, a thief, a harlot, an adulteress, a lesbian, a murderer, a coveter, a backbiter, a gossiper, a manipulator, a deceiver. This sinfulness all went away when you truly repented of your past and were buried with Christ in water baptism.

I admire Bible teacher Joyce Meyer. She faced up to all of the brokenness caused in her life by her father's sexual abuse of her when she was young. Most women feel tremendous guilt from this type of molestation, even though they were the victims. They have trouble with ever forgiving the person that abused them, and often have trouble in relationship with their husbands. Meyer, however, has chosen to not only allow God to heal her and help her through her anger and unforgiveness, but she decided along the way that it was too important for God to be able to use her in women's ministry to hold onto those hindrances. She let go of the hurt, and so must we --all of it. We have to obey God to be used by God. Let go of the hurt and let Him heal you. Let go of the unforgiveness and release the forgiveness of God to yourself and others.

Satan will not give up on reminding you of your past, because he has had such success with this wile in crippling us from doing God's work and living victorious lives. None of us want to be counted among the brothers and sisters who want to give you the evil eye, to let the broken among you know that we know all about you. None of us want to be the hypocrites making sure everyone else knows all about the past of our brothers and sisters. We expect the sinner to talk against us, but when our brothers and sisters do this, our walk with God gets a little boggy. If any of us have been guilty of speaking ill against our sisters in the Lord, we need to repent (meaning ask God to forgive us and never be guilty of that again). We have to love and forgive one another. We do not want to do damage to babies in Christ by telling everyone all about the sins they are coming out of; we want to pray for them in our private prayer closets that they will keep the overcoming power of Jesus Christ alive in their lives. None of us should be guilty of crippling the walk of a new Christian. I feel like I need to elaborate on this a minute.

Christian women have trouble coming together because of a lack of trust. In the world, we had people who broke our trust, and if we are honest with ourselves, we broke the trust of some of our friends along the way. We need to be able to trust one another when we come into the family of God. If everyone was a grown up Christian immediately, we could do so, but there is a time period to grow in the grace of God, so we let one another down sometimes, and hence, Jesus tells us to forgive one another. It is so important that you grow up quickly, however, so you do not do damage to your Christian family. We should not talk about one another; we should not turn our heads when we see a sister in town and not speak to her; we should not exclude any sister from our events; we should not roll our eyes when a sister walks by who isn't quite on our spiritual level yet, who is, in fact, failing the Lord. We are instructed to pray for her, to go to her in love with correction. We do not judge unless we wish to be judged!

We do not want to condemn anyone else, and we do not want to condemn ourselves. I know from experience that we can get on a roller coaster in our living for God if we keep going around the condemnation mountain. I remember one minister helping me with a beautiful sermon that he did on "Living in a Haunted House." He pointed out that God has forgiven us sometimes, but we keep ourselves in a haunted house, reviewing some evil that we did in our past, hence staying in condemnation because we cannot forgive ourselves. We have to pray for the Lord to help us to forgive ourselves and others. We are all needed in the harvest today--there is no more time for condemnation. If you are staying bowed down with condemnation, the only ones you are pleasing are Satan and your human accusers. Jesus wants you to believe in the victory He won for you on Calvary. It was a complete victory; when you claim His salvation, the old girl is dead, and the babe in Christ needs to grow up and get busy doing kingdom work.

To move forward as soldiers of the cross, we must release the condemnation of Satan, ourselves, and the world. We must confess the Word to stay victorious over this condemnation. **II Corinthians 5:17** is a good scripture to memorize for this purpose. **"Therefore, if any man is in Christ, he is a new creature, old things are passed away, ALL things are become new."** Besides condemnation hindering us in our faith walk, we sometimes must let go of hurt and the memory of hurt. There is a saying that "Time heals all wounds." Sometimes, however, time just keeps revisiting those wounds and they fester, rather than heal. I know there are women that have had all manner of abuses committed against them in the past, and also have memory of sinfulness they committed against others. It is time to get a release from the hurt and the memory. Jesus loves us too much to want us to be burdened down with the terribleness of some of our pasts. If you keep a wall up in your heart, there is a part of you that cannot be available to minister to others, and he has called us out to minister to others. As a matter of fact, he is calling us out to minister to those who have been hurt in the same area we have been hurt. Some things cannot be talked about to anyone but God. That is just wisdom. You do need to give the hurt and the memory to God to get your healing. Some of you have had to deal with the memory of molestation from your past, be it from a family member or a neighbor. Let the memory go and let go of the unforgiveness to get the healing you need to move forward. Besides cases of molestation, some of us may have committed fornication or adultery, and we feel inadequate to be used in God's kingdom because of the condemnation we keep on ourselves. If you had an abortion, put a child up for adoption, divorced several times, committed a terrible act against someone else that cost them dearly, maybe an act of betrayal, you can live in a haunted house. You don't want to think about it, talk about it. Listen, Jesus hates the sin, but Jesus loves you. You have confessed your sins to God, and when you repented, you started walking God's way. He doesn't even remember your past. Scripture says, **"As far as the east is from the west, so far has he removed our transgression from us." (Psalm 103:12)** Some of you need to believe that, and let go of the memories that are haunting you. If you refuse to forgive yourself or someone else that has hurt you, Jesus said in a parable about the debtor that you cannot be forgiven until you forgive.

Do you want to lock up God's mercy and blessing because you refuse to forgive someone who molested or betrayed you? That is what you are doing if you hold onto unforgiveness. Do you want to be a bold witness for God and help save souls? Anointing will never rest on condemnation. If you do not stop letting Satan, yourself, and others place condemnation back on you for things that God has chosen to forget, you are never going to go forward as the soldiers in Christ's army that you are supposed to be.

In the book of Mark, Mary, the sister of Martha and Lazarus, demonstrates her love of Jesus in washing his feet and anointing them with a precious oil. One of the disciples complains that this could have been sold and given to the poor. In Luke, a woman in Bethany is attending to Jesus in this way. This was a common courtesy to provide water to wash the feet of your guest. Perhaps it is the same woman in Luke, but she is unnamed in Luke. Let us consider this text that memorializes an unnamed woman in scripture--a woman who had great faith and love for the master.

Week Two Woman of Faith
An Unnamed Woman

"And, behold, a woman in the city, which was a sinner, when she knew that Jesus sat at meat in the Pharisee's house, brought an alabaster box of ointment, And stood at his feet behind him weeping, and began to wash his feet with tears, and did wipe them with the hairs of her head, and kissed his feet, and anointed them with the ointment. Now when the Pharisee which had bidden him saw it, he spake within himself, saying, This man, if he were a prophet, would have known who and what manner of woman this is that toucheth him: for she is a sinner. And Jesus answering said unto him, Simon, I have somewhat to say unto thee. And he saith, Master, say on. There was a certain creditor which had two debtors: the one owed five hundred pence, and the other fifty. And when they had nothing to pay, he frankly forgave them both. Tell me therefore, which of them will love him most? Simon answered and said, I suppose that he, to whom he forgave most. And he said unto him, Thou hast rightly judged. And he turned to the woman, and said unto Simon, Seest thou this woman? I entered into thine house, thou gavest me no water for my feet; but she hath washed my feet with tears, and wiped them with the hairs of her head. Thou gavest me no kiss. But this woman since the time I came in hath not ceased to kiss my feet. My head with oil thou didst not anoint: but this woman hath anointed my feet with ointment. Wherefore I say unto thee, Her sins, which are many, are forgiven; for she loved much. But to whom little is forgiven, the same loveth little." (Luke 7:37-47)

Faith in and love for the master are evident in this unnamed woman. She knows what is coming to Jesus, doesn't she? She is anointing him with a precious ointment that is usually a gift to kings. She is weeping and kissing his feet and wiping his feet with her hair. She is totally forgetting about herself and what Simon, (who is appalled that Jesus is allowing this sinner woman to even touch him) is thinking. She has come to worship Jesus, to thank Jesus, to serve Jesus, without thought of herself or how she looks to others. You will not be effectual in ministering God's grace to others until you forget about what you look like to others.

I attend a church sometimes that has a woman in it who worships and praises God at every point in the service that it will not be out of order for her to do so. I don't know everything the Lord has brought her through, but I know without a doubt that she loves Jesus and she doesn't care if the President comes in the church; she will be praising Him.

I know that we have all witnessed people who raise themselves up as righteous and look down on others. We all know things about the people in our hometown and we sift that information through our brains and we label people. We decide who is a sinner and how bad their sin is sometimes, don't we? Jesus is not even condemning the people that some of us would shun to be around, and is frowning heavily at some of us in church who are not embracing the sinners in our hurting world to help them get to Jesus and stay with Jesus. The Word of God says that grace abounds where sin abounds. We are not to be walking in and practicing sin once we get into the church. However, many of us had sin abounding in our lives before we got into church. His grace has abounded to us. We should not make that grace of none effect by walking around cast down. We should be worshipping and loving Jesus and walking in all of the grace He has given us, operating in the purpose He wants us to walk in. Why don't you lay down the condemnation for good, and walk into your purpose today? I am one of those women who love Jesus much; I am well aware of all that he has delivered me from, and I just love him and want to obey and serve him. We all want to be a vessel that the Lord can use, don't we? Realize that you are loosed from your past. Just let it go. You really were loosed from it all when you came to Christ.

What I Can Learn from the Alabaster Box Story!

1. Jesus loves me just the way I am.

2. I owe Him my life and service.

3. I owe Him continual praise.

4. If Jesus does not condemn me, who am I, who is Satan, who is anyone else to try and condemn me?

5. Jesus wants us to love the worst sinners to Him to be saved.

6. We are not to judge anyone!

No matter how broken or bruised we are, like the reed he will not cast out, or no matter how out of desire you may feel from being hurt through church, through church members, God can fan a flame in us; He can take the hurt away. He can mend our broken hearts. He can use each one of us, no matter what our past has been. We never want to stand in the way of God using anyone by thinking that we don't want that person used because of his/her past. God knows what He is doing. Let him use you, and everyone that may need to know this--don't stand in the way of a sister being used by the Lord because of your bad attitude toward people you may consider less than you. That isn't really an attitude that God is accepting of; he received the sinner's prayer, remember, not the Pharisee's that stood denouncing the sinner, bragging about his fasting and alms. Jesus said that the sinner went away justified, not the Pharisee. We don't see things the way that God does. He looks on our hearts and He does not despise our sin and brokenness. He just asks us to repent and sin no more.

God is calling us to get off the pew and to get out to the harvest. I challenge you to reach out this week to one person. I challenge you to let go of past hurts, past memories that are harmful, unforgiveness of those who have betrayed your trust. Let it go! Let it go right now!

I remember seeking for the Holy Ghost for about three years. I would wear out the saints at the altar. I thought in my mind that I must be the worst sinner ever and that God just would never give me that gift. I was lying by my little boy one day (He needed me to lay by him to go to sleep). I was asking God, "Why have I not received the Holy Ghost yet?" He answered me! Here is what He said. "I have all of these blessings stored up for you, but you have kept me from giving them to you because of your unforgiveness. Whatever is bound on the earth shall be bound in heaven. Whatever is loosed on the earth shall be loosed in heaven." I understood immediately. I said, "Lord, I know that I keep telling you that I am forgiving that person, but I also know that in my heart I haven't. I don't know that I can. Can you do that through me somehow?" He did. You may be like me and you don't even know how to let go of the unforgiveness even though you want to do so. I am telling you that God *can* do it for you, just like He can give you love for others that you can never have in your human state. Let God forgive through you, and let him baptize you with a love for people that you have never felt before. I don't understand how He does it, but I know He helped me to forgive, and shortly after that day, I received the baptism of the Holy Ghost. The woman who has been forgiven so much is the one who is able to love the Lord so much. God had forgiven me of so much, it didn't even make sense for me to be holding on to unforgiveness against someone else, but I was. We need to be so in love with our Savior who has forgiven us so much, and we need to love even those who don't know how to love. I blocked the wonderful blessing of receiving the gift of the Holy Ghost for a number of years because I felt justified in holding onto unforgiveness.

Some things that have been done to us are unfair and unjust, but we still do not get to be the judge, and we must remember the unjust and unfair and wrong things that we have done to others. God has so much He wants to do for us and through us. Isn't it worth that to just let go of the hurt and unforgiveness? Trust me, you will enjoy the liberty you will be able to walk in. Bruised people can be healed, and terrible wounds can be healed. The wound may leave a scar, but it does not have to remain open or get festered where we keep picking at it, or allow it to become infected. Jesus is the healer of our pasts. He says to give it all to Him. He will heal even the memory of the pain of your abuse or your bad decisions if you let Him. If you wish to help others to recover themselves, you need to be healed by Him. Those of you who used to have a serious prayer life and your heart was burdened for others, but you have allowed the cares of life and trials of life to distract you from your purpose, Jesus is fanning the smoldering flax; He is here to fan the flame of passion for Him and His work back into your lives. In Revelation, one of the churches is warned to return to their first love. This caution is for each of us individually. We are to be on fire in love with our Savior! It isn't hard to be passionate about something when you love it. How much do you love Jesus today? Do you love Him enough to obey Him and do whatever He asks you to do? Are you sold out?

> "Bruised people can be healed, and terrible wounds can be healed."

If you are reading this and you haven't received Jesus as your Savior, please believe in your heart that Jesus is the Son of God, and ask forgiveness for the sins you have committed against him. Find a believing Bible church, and get baptized in Jesus name and seek to be filled with His Spirit. If you have hurt you can't get past or unforgiveness to someone in your heart, let go of it so you can receive the blessings that God is holding for you. Find an altar, and what I want you to lay on that altar is the memory of hurt. I want you to touch your altar with your hand, close your eyes a moment, and release forgiveness of a specific person, a betrayal, a hurt from your children. Lay it on the altar and don't pick it back up. Just let go of the hurt, the betrayal, the unforgiveness, and let Jesus heal that so you can be released to victory in your walk with Jesus.

Pray this aloud: Father, I want to give you all of the praise and glory for what you have done, are doing, and will be doing in my life. I know that you are drawing me into something bigger and better for my life than I could ever even imagine on my own. I am asking you to help me to understand how I may be blocking my own supernatural favor from you when I do not ask for your guidance, when I do not give you all the cares of my life, when I do not trust you to help me to forgive and love completely, everyone, every day. I know that you have brought me out of a pit that I was dangling over, Lord, and that you have set me on the firm foundation of your Word. Help me to study and embrace your Word, so that as you make divine appointments in my life to help others, that Word will come forth from the deep recesses of my heart where I have hid it, so that I would not sin against you. From this time forth, help me to lead others to a real knowledge of who you

are, to teach them how faithful you are to forgive us, and help me to forgive others. I am asking you to heal all emotional wounds in me today, heal the memory of abuse, of molestation. Father, help me to forgive myself if I am keeping condemnation alive within me over some terrible sin I did in my past that in my humanness I do not feel I have the right to be forgiven for; Lord, you have proven you are a big God to us in saving us, healing us, and delivering us. Help me to have the boldness and confidence to release the power you have placed in me to serve others and to draw others to you by expressing your love to others daily. Thank you for loving me and holding me in your care. You said that I could ask you for wisdom and I am. Increase my knowledge, increase my understanding of your Word, and increase my faith more and more, Father. In Jesus name I pray. Amen.

Remember to do your worksheets, to do your challenge this week, and to do your memorization of verses to quote when the storms and tests show up. If you start asking God specifically to lead you in talking to specific people, or asking Him for specific needs, beginning to supplicate in earnest for the spiritual needs of your church, you will begin to see Him answering the prayers. I want to emphasize to do the challenges and answer honestly all questions in the worksheets if you wish to truly see growth in overcoming hindrances, and growth in increasing and acting on your faith.

As you move from week to week, mentally review what you think you were meant to learn each week and check yourself to see if you did apply the lesson and you are applying the challenges. If your hindrances are not removed, you will never walk in the full boldness the Lord means for you to be walking in to reach the lost.

WEEK TWO WORKSHEETS

Overcoming Hurt Caused by Others and Ourselves

"That it might be fulfilled that was spoken by Esais, the prophet, saying, Behold my servant, whom I have chosen, my beloved, in whom my soul is well pleased: I will put my spirit upon him, and he will shew judgment to the Gentiles. He shall not strive nor cry, nor shall any man hear his voice in the streets. A bruised reed shall he not break, and smoking flax shall he not quench, till he send forth judgment unto victory. Matthew 12:17-21

Notes:

____

____

____

____

How have I been bruised?

____

____

How have I been broken?

____

____

Have I bruised or broken someone else? Confess it here.

____

____

Am I coals that need to be fanned into commitment for Jesus?

____

____

Am I smoldering and just need a renewing of the Holy Ghost to blow through my spirit to catch fire for God?

____

____

Am I studying the Word, praying and watching for my soul, and interceding for others? Am I on fire and ready to light others with the gospel of Jesus Christ?

____

____

"And straightening up, Jesus says, Woman where are they? Did no one condemn thee? And she said, No one, Lord. Neither do I condemn you; go your way; From now on sin no more." (John 8: 10-11)

Notes:

____

____

____

____

Examine whether you see yourself as this sinful woman, or as those condemning her, or as Jesus, just wanting her to be saved and come out of sin? Be honest with yourself and give the wrong attitude to Jesus. Ask him to help you love and have the compassion and mercy He has for others.

____

____

____

____

"There is therefore now no condemnation to those who are in Christ Jesus. Therefore, if any man be in Christ, he is a new creature: old things are passed away, ALL things are become new."(II Corinthians 5:17)

Week Two Woman of Faith
An unnamed woman
Luke 7:37-47

Notes:

____

____

____

____

How comfortable are you with praising God in front of others?

____

____

Are you uncomfortable with demonstrative worship?

____

____

Why?

____

____

Are you offended by it or do you believe God is offended by it?

____

____

Why?

____

____

Do you understand servanthood? (We must decrease--He must increase).

____

____

**"It is not this way among you, but whoever wishes to become great among you shall become your servant."
Matthew 20:26**

Are you a sold-out subject of Jesus Christ as this woman was?

____

____

Or, are you still skeptical, but open to instruction as Simon was?

____

____

Are you convinced that God loves you just as much as anyone, that He can use you in any capacity that He chooses, and that He is no respecter of persons?

____

____

____

Write down what you are going to do to keep from being defeated by the following:

Fear:

____

____

Negativity: (yours and others)

____

____

Condemnation:

____

____

Are you hindering your service to the Lord by holding onto unforgiveness? Write the names of those you have unforgiveness or condemnation against here and ask God to help you release them to Him.

____

____

____

____

Do you feel the Lord planting something in your heart to do for Him? Don't say anything yet to anyone. Just record the thought or desire that has come to your heart recently and pray and ask God about it this week.

___

___

___

Examine your feelings about the following:

Girls who are pregnant out of wedlock:

___

___

People immersed in immorality (multiple sexual experiences, homosexuality, pornography)

___

___

People bound by drugs, alcohol:

___

___

People bound by gambling:

___

___

People bound by shopping, spending, food disorders:

___

___

Women who have had an abortion:

___

___

Child molesters/other molesters:

___

___

Thieves/liars/murderers:

____

____

We all know that all of the preceding is sin, but are we looking at the people who commit the sins in a different way than the Lord would? Are we to be like Jesus? Now, look at them through Jesus' eyes--are they all sinners in need of His love, forgiveness, and acceptance?

____

____

Weren't you a sinner, too, when He saved you?

____

____

Are you willing to get your attitudes right to please Jesus? To keep a unified church body that can love souls to Christ?

____

____

Ask yourself this: Why would anyone want to become a Christian like us if what they see is backbiting, judgment, criticism, and condemnation among the Christians?

____

____

"By this shall all men know that ye are my disciples, if ye have love one to another." John 13:35

We all have different strengths of personalities; we all came to God with different sinfulness; we all have different talents. Can we love, support, and encourage one another so that others will want to come to Jesus? Write down an area you think you need to work on to show more the love of Christ.

____

____

____

What needs to change in you to promote a healthy church and to give glory to God so sinners will come to the light?

____

____

What fearful thought or negative feeling is keeping your light still under the bushel basket?

____

____

What part of the light bulb needs cleaning?

____

____

Who needs your light this week?

____

____

Do you know how to share this gospel with someone? Are you following traditions you have heard or the Word of God when you explain the salvation message?

____

____

This Week's Challenges

1. When you hear a good report, say: "Praise the Lord! Hallelujah!" out loud.

2. When you are alone in your house, dance before the Lord and thank Him for helping to deliver you out of fear, negativity, and condemnation (praising and thanking in faith until you feel it). I know some of you have never done this, but scripture tells us that "He inhabits the praise of His people." Do you want to enter His presence? Try this.

3. Before you enter the house of God where you attend worship services, say out loud, "Thank you for the great things you have done and are still doing for me, Jesus! You are greatly to be praised. I love you and adore you!" (At least praise Him in your car as you pull up to the church. You

will be astonished at how you begin to feel the Lord when you direct your worship to Him, instead of walking into His sanctuary only wanting Him to bless you). He instructed us to enter His courts with thanksgiving. Enter your prayer sessions this way too.

4. Look around daily to see the problems of others. Look for the right opportunity with the right person and say, "May I do something for you?" Ask the Lord to work between you. They may open up to you. Let them share. Ask them if they would like you to pray for them. When they say, "Yes," take their hand and pray a simple, fervent prayer for their need, thanking Jesus for the blessing and care you know He will take over them. If a woman, ask her to have lunch with you. If you are struggling financially, you may need to fast a meal or two, or fast a treat you are used to having to be able to do this. God will reward your obedience and sacrifice. Don't tell anyone what you are doing. Just start obeying God. This is that "bread you are casting on the water."

Notes:

If any of the above makes you uncomfortable, ask yourself why, and write it here.

____

____

____

____

Memory Verse

"There is therefore now no condemnation to those who are in Christ Jesus. Therefore, if any man be in Christ, he is a new creature: old things are passed away, ALL things are become new." (II Corinthians 5:17)

WEEK THREE

Overcoming Unforgiveness

Thus far, we should have begun to work on overcoming fear, negativity, and hurt caused by ourselves and others. This week's lesson will carry on with some of what we began to discuss in week two's lesson. Unforgiveness: I know that unforgiveness is a big hurdle to get past to open up the blessings God has for us, and I want to deal more with unforgiveness because of the hindrance it will be to your Christian walk, hindering you from being released into your purpose for the things of God. It is so important to understand this one thing today: you cannot receive the mercy of God as long as you are not giving mercy to others.

Pray for God to open your eyes to how important forgiveness is in your walk, and ask that He would help you to forgive anyone from your past that you have a grudge against, or to forgive any sister or brother in the Lord who may have caused you hurt.

> **Pray this aloud: Father, I approach the throne of grace realizing that great mercy has been shown to me that I can even come before you claiming to be part of the family of God. You have made me a daughter of the most high God because of your grace and mercy and the atonement you took care of on the cross of Calvary. There is absolutely nothing I can do to receive your mercy that you extended to me from that cross. I realize that following the receiving of that work in my life, I am supposed to extend love and mercy to**

others, and in not doing so, I am blocking blessings and mercy from you, and am needlessly living in torment. In my humanness, I realize that I can never give the kind of love and forgiveness that you have shown to me. I realize that I need you supernaturally helping me to lay down every wrong feeling, thought, attitude, grudge, hurt, misunderstanding that I may have against others in my life. I do not want to block the blessings you have for me, God. Search my heart, oh God! Help me to truly examine today where I stand in forgiving others. If there is a place in my heart with a wall of unforgiveness or hardness toward anyone, reveal that to me, and melt my resistance with your loving Spirit. Do in me what I cannot do in myself. I am asking you to baptize me with love and mercy as I go about serving you. I am thankful that you have forgotten my past and forgiven me. Help me to always forget others pasts, to pray for those who would use me or speak ill against me, and to release everyone in my life, past and present, to your judgment and mercy, that I will not have judgment placed against me for being disobedient in this area. Give me a gift of mercy, if you will, Lord. In Jesus name. Amen

Consider the following scriptures:

"Therefore is the kingdom of heaven likened unto a certain king, which would take account of his servants. And when he had begun to reckon, one was brought unto him, which owed him ten thousand talents. But forasmuch as he had not to pay, his lord commanded him to be sold, and his wife, and children, and all that he had, and payment to be made. The servant therefore fell down, and worshipped him, saying Lord, have patience with me, and I will pay thee all. Then the lord of that servant was moved with compassion, and loosed him, and forgave him the debt. But the same servant went out, and found one of his fellow servants, which owed him an hundred pence, and he laid hands on him, and took (him) by the throat, saying, Pay me that thou owest. And his fellow servant fell down at his feet, and besought him, saying, Have patience with me, and I will pay thee all. And he would not: but went and cast him into prison, till he should pay the debt. So when his fellow servants saw what was done, they were very sorry, and came and told unto their lord all that was done. Then his lord, after that he had called him, said unto him, O thou wicked servant, I forgave thee all that debt, because thou desiredst me. Shouldest not thou also have had compassion on thy fellow servant, even as I had pity on thee? And his lord was wroth, and he delivered him to the tormentors, till he should pay all that was due unto him. So likewise shall my heavenly Father do also unto you, if ye from your hearts forgive not every one his brother their trespasses." (Matthew 18:23-35)

This parable really comes down to an illustration of entering the kingdom of heaven. God has extended salvation to us, but we learn from scriptures that we can block some mercy and blessings when we are disobedient in forgiving others their trespasses against us. What do we need to do to be forgiven? What does it take to come into the kingdom of heaven? What must we do to be saved? When the Jews asked Peter concerning this on the day of Pentecost, we see recorded in **Acts 2:38**, Peter, sharing the "key to the kingdom" that had been revealed to him. **"Repent, and be baptized, every one of you in the name of Jesus Christ for the remission of sins and ye shall receive the gift of the Holy Ghost."** This is what God offers to humanity, a humanity that betrayed Him when he walked on earth, but a humanity that he went to the cross for to atone for the sins of a sinful world that had committed every manner of crime and betrayal against him. He said, "Father, forgive them."

Before we go any further, let us examine the Acts 2:38 scripture that we have heard so many times. It is really the initial scripture given to begin the New Testament church. Following the 120 being baptized with the Holy Ghost in the upper room experience, seventeen nationalities of people are in the audience of Peter and the disciples, many of those the very Jews whom had cried, "Crucify him!" Now they know that Jesus did come out of the grave and ascended into heaven, and now they know they need to be saved. How can they be? What an ultimate act of mercy from God, absolute unconditional love from the Father to His creation, that the salvation message is for them, too.

Peter, standing with the eleven, tells them the salvation message of Acts 2:38. Peter is the one whom Jesus gave the keys to the kingdom because the Spirit of God had shown Peter who Jesus was. Peter gives us the key to the kingdom when he gives us Acts 2:38. To repent means to turn. What do we turn from when we come to the saving knowledge of our need to let Jesus become Lord of our life? We turn from worldly thinking, we turn from sinful lifestyles, we turn from hateful attitudes, and we take on a servant attitude like the one that Jesus illustrated to us when he walked on earth. We say "I'm sorry for my sins and my messed up life, Lord. I want to learn your ways and walk in them. I want to obey you."

What does God do at this point? He forgives us. We follow our repentance by being baptized in the name of the Lord Jesus Christ for the remission of our sins. When we are baptized in Jesus name, Acts 2:38 states that our sins are remitted. That means that our sins are done away with, forever. They can't come back. God put them away from us as far as the east is from the west. Think about what some of those sins were just for a moment. I would not encourage anyone to think about their past very often, (you remember from last week that that is Satan's and self-righteous people's job), because I want to encourage us to walk in the new life and think on good things at all times, but just for a moment, remember the people you betrayed, the sins you led others to commit with you, the lies you told, the times you stole, the people you murdered with your hateful lies and backstabbing. Now, consider how much God forgave you. Consider your own heart and what you are holding against someone, and maybe it is a terrible, terrible betrayal of your innocence; maybe that thing you are holding in your heart is a terrible injustice against you or a loved one. God said, "Vengeance is mine…I will repay." We are not God.

We may see the injustice and be able to judge that it is wrong what someone has done, but what we cannot see is the heart of man and when it may change and turn to God. Only God needs to judge. If He chooses to give someone mercy, that is His right. You can only hurt yourself holding onto unforgiveness and withholding mercy from others. Why? Because God will withhold His mercy from you until you learn to release mercy to others. Jesus did a complete work on the cross of Calvary, atoning for the sins of the world. He can't take that back. However, we do not receive that work done on Calvary until we come to the foot of the cross, repent, and confess Jesus as Lord. So, does God take that forgiveness away that we receive at the foot of the cross when we are refusing to forgive and show mercy to others? No. However, we all know that when we sin, we are adjured to come again through our mediator, Jesus Christ, and repent again over any sin we have in our life. Repent also means to turn, not just say "we are sorry." We cannot be forgiven of those daily sinful deeds and attitudes until we confess them and turn from them. Unforgiveness is sin. To hold it inside of us, to not confess it to God, to not turn from it, or repent of it, is sin. Sin keeps us from God. Sin blocks our relationship with God. Unconfessed sin leaves us feeling not quite right, unclean, and prevents us from going boldly to the throne of grace. I choose to deal with "overcoming unforgiveness" because it is really a stronghold of Satan's in our lives. Keeping unforgiveness in our heart, refusing to be merciful to those around us who are sinners, is what causes the body of Christ to be accused of hypocrisy by the world, and what causes many people to avoid coming to church. Think right now, "Is there anyone in the world who believes that I have wrong thoughts and hard feelings toward them and that would make my church the last place they would want to show up to worship God? Is there anyone you would not want to worship God with you? If there is, you have a problem with unforgiveness and are keeping the mercy of God bound not only from that person, but bound from yourself also. I shared a story in last week's lesson about when God spoke to me about unforgiveness. Let me remind you of it.

"Unforgiveness is Sin"

After I had repented and been baptized in Jesus name, I began to seek the Holy Ghost infilling that I had read in the Word I could have, and I had witnessed other people receiving. For about three years, I wore saints out at the altar. Every church service, I would go to the altar and seek for this gift. I had finally about decided that I had just been too bad in my BC days to be a candidate for this baptism. I was lying by my youngest son one day in his bed, turned on my side (he had to have me lay by him to go to sleep). I asked the Lord why I had not been filled with the Holy Ghost. He answered me, in a voice so clear, that I thought it was audible, but I guess it was just a very loud spirit voice. He said, "I have all of these blessings stored up for you, but you cannot receive them because of your unforgiveness. Whatever is bound on earth shall be bound in heaven, and whatever is loosed on earth shall be loosed in heaven." I said, "I know what you are talking about, Lord. I have said that I have forgiven that person, and I believe that I want to forgive that person, but I know in my heart that I have not. I don't know whether I can. Can you do that through me? Can you forgive through me? I know this sounds different, but He melted my heart then, and helped me to forgive that person. It was a very short time before I received the baptism of the Holy Ghost that I had been seeking. You may have been hurt terribly in the past, or you may live in a circumstance that requires daily forgiveness, or sad though it is, we may have to forgive brothers and sisters in the Lord who are still carnal and have done us wrong, talking about us. God can help us to forgive and He can help us to love His way. He did it through me, and I know He will do it through you if you are having a hard time letting go of something.

Allow me to share a few scriptures with you that may shine the light on why it is so important for you to let go of any unforgiveness, if you want to please God and do the work He wants you to do. Are we only wanting to make it to heaven, or are we wanting to help save others from the pit of hell? If we don't get our walk right, we are never going to be able to help others to get saved. **Mark 11:24 and 25** says, **"Therefore I say unto you, what things soever ye desire, when ye pray, believe that ye receive them, and ye shall have them. And when ye stand praying, forgive, if ye have ought (something) against any, that your Father also which is in heaven may forgive you your trespasses."** It sounds like His forgiveness of our sins is bound if we do not release forgiveness to others for their sins, doesn't it? That is exactly what that scripture is saying. Do you need to release forgiveness to someone? Do that now.

"…Lest any root of bitterness springing up trouble you, and thereby many be defiled." (Hebrews 12:15). The definition of "defiled" is "morally blemished, unclean, impure." (Webster's) Jesus says that He is coming for a church without spot or blemish. We cannot have bitterness or unforgivensss in our hearts and believe that we will be raised up to be with Jesus one day. He would have to go against His Word, and He is not going to do that, so it is us that must line up with the Word, examine ourselves, and pray for the Lord to help us purify ourselves in these areas. Let me read **I John 3:14, "We know that we have passed from death unto life, because we love the brethren. He that loveth not his brother abideth in death."** Jesus came to bring us life and that more abundantly, but we can't walk in abundant life if we are not showing love to our brothers and sisters. He says that we are, in fact, "abiding in death."

> "Jesus is coming for a church without spot or blemish."

In our parable from Matthew, we see that the lord delivered the man to the tormentors. That last scripture: **Matthew 18:35 says "…likewise shall my heavenly Father do also unto you, if ye from your hearts forgive not every one his brother their trespasses."** Do you know people who are living in torment today? Are you living in torment? Forgive.

**Let's recap how costly *unforgiveness is for us:*
**
> We cannot receive God's forgiveness as long as we are being unforgiving.

> We cannot receive the blessings He wants us to have.

> We cannot be spiritually fruitful because love can't flow through an unforgiving spirit.

> We cannot pass from spiritual death and enter relationship again with the Father.

> We cannot say we love God if we *aren't* keeping His commandments.

> We cannot abide in Christ's love and be a blessing to anyone else.

The Lord said that we know the body of Christ by the fruit they produce, by the love they have to one another. What fruit are we supposed to produce? We have an explanation of this fruit. Galatians 5:22-23 lists nine attributes of one fruit of the spirit. They are "love, joy, peace, patience, kindness, goodness, faithfulness, gentleness, and self-control. Against such things there is no law." You can't say, "I have six of these fruits and am working on the other three, because they are not plural. The Spirit is one, and we are supposed to produce all nine attributes, so when you received the Holy Ghost, you received the Spirit to produce all nine. Just let them produce. Do not nullify what the Spirit of God is trying to produce in you by spoiling the fruit with bad attitudes, lack of mercy, unforgiveness, and disobedience to the Spirit of God. Obey God and forgive that the blessings of God are released into your life, and that the fruit we see is good fruit, fruit that others want.

I think we can see how unforgiveness and lack of mercy cannot release these attributes from us to others--to **all others.** God has instructed us to not allow a root of bitterness to spring up in our lives. That root will damage the fruit. We all must realize that we cannot produce good fruit unless we stay connected to the vine. We are the branches. We are what the fruit hangs on. We hold the fruit for others to see. We are dead branches with spoiled fruit, however, if we do not allow the vine, which is the Holy Spirit of God and the Word of God to continually flow through us and feed us. Continually! Remember that God said, **"If ye abide in me, and my words abide in you, ye shall ask what ye will, and it shall be done unto you." (John 15:7)** I have presented this verse before, but it is essential to understand what God is saying here if we want to become the powerful Christians that it is His will we should become. We do not do anything on our own. Before we begin our day, we should have praised God, asked Him to guide our steps for the day, to give us wisdom and discernment, and opportunities to witness. We should be checking in with Him all day as the world encroaches and begins to try and steal our joy and peace. We should go "into that secret place with Him" that no one and no law of man can take from us. The law may say "no prayer in school;" well, I confess to being a lawbreaker. I must continually go to God during my day to step back into peace and calm. If I didn't, I would not be showing any fruit of the spirit to my classes many times. I can't produce good fruit without abiding in Him. Can you? Can you hold your tongue when someone gets in your face, or someone is lying about you? Are you chasing around trying to take vengeance on everyone who has ever done you wrong, making sure that you have told everyone the wrong that has been done to you, or are you operating as Jesus did when He was on earth? He just said, "Whatever you say."(paraphrasing) He appeared totally unmoved by their lying, their mocking, their rejection. He did not retaliate. He was so hooked up with the will of the Father that he was not turned by the distractions. Did he feel hurt? Yes. He always prayed and asked the Father to forgive them. People have no idea what they are doing when they come against the anointed people of God. Just abide in Him, read His Word, and continually go to Him in prayer. Finish your day thanking Him for keeping you, for instructing you, for providing opportunities to witness, for giving you the words of wisdom that spoke to someone's heart that day, that gave them healing, that gave them encouragement.

Produce good fruit.

Do you want to give everyone bruised fruit? No. Let go of the past and present hurts. Forgive, so you can be healed, and so you can take the Word of God and His healing to the broken and bruised of this world who need the same healing. Forgive. Right now! Just let it go. Ask God to help you. He will. Do you know what happens usually when one person gets locked into unforgiveness? It begins to infect all those around them, just like a rotten apple or rotten potato in a bag begins to rot those around it. If we don't forgive, we are not just going to cost ourselves mercy, but we will also cause a great cost to those around us.

> "Bruised fruit will begin to rot those around it."

Do you have any idea how exciting the body of Christ could be and how many souls could be won for the Lord if we obeyed in extending mercy and forgiveness to every person we come in contact with, if we obeyed in walking in love to everyone, to every single person we come in contact with, those who have talked about us, those who have betrayed us, those who have stabbed us in the back, those who roll their eyes at us, those who make sure we see how they disapprove of us, those who are rank sinners, those who smell bad, those who make us uncomfortable? Do you think God doesn't understand our human reaction to all of these things? He does. Jesus knew that Judas had sold him out for thirty pieces of silver, but when Judas kissed him on the cheek to let the soldiers know who Jesus was, Jesus addressed Judas as "Friend." He did not accuse him or deliver an angry tirade against this man. He is well aware that in and of ourselves we can never love and forgive in the way He is commanding us to love and forgive. So, how do we do it? We get full of the Spirit of God. The Holy Ghost will give us the love, the joy, and the power to obey God in loving and forgiving. The Holy Ghost spreads the love of God abroad in our hearts. We are instructed not to let a root of bitterness spring up in our hearts. That would spoil our fruit, wouldn't it?

Week Three Woman of Faith
Naomi

I am choosing to speak of Naomi this week. She represents the overcoming we all must do to get past bitterness. She represents backsliding we need to return from; she represents coming back to the one true God and bringing someone else to the knowledge of our kinsman/redeemer. She represents bringing someone who does not know the one true God into fellowship and salvation, and into purpose. I want us to lead others to a saving knowledge of Jesus Christ and it is my hope that we will all discover our purpose (if we are not already walking in it) while we are studying the Word of God and seeking His direction.

"So Boaz took Ruth, and she was his wife: and when he went in unto her, the Lord gave her conception, and she bare a son. And the women said unto Naomi, Blessed be the Lord, which hath not left thee this day without a kinsman, that his name may be famous in Israel. And he shall be unto thee a restorer of thy life, and a nourisher of thine old age: for thy daughter-in-law, which loveth thee, which is better to thee than seven sons, hath borne him. And Naomi took the child, and laid it in her bosom, and became nurse unto it. And the women her neighbours gave it a name, saying, There is a son born to Naomi; and they called his name Obed: he is the father of Jesse, the father of David. (Ruth 4:13-17)

We are reading the good outcome of a bad situation. Naomi decides to move from bitterness to receiving restoration of a good life through a kinsman/redeemer. Naomi means "gracious." Naomi, however, chooses to rename herself after life's circumstances come against her. She goes from Naomi, or "gracious" to Mara, or "bitter." From the time she leaves Bethlehem (which means House of Bread) until she returns, she has some very bitter circumstances occur. Anyone who has ever backslid from their close place in God understands bitter circumstances, when we have taken ourselves out of the hand of God. No one else can take us out of His hand, but we can remove ourselves. Naomi and her husband leave Bethlehem during a famine to go into the land of the Moabites for provision. I have trouble believing that God meant for them to depend on the Moabite people for their sustenance. Israel had already lost sons and daughters through intermarriage with these people who would get the Israelites to forget their God and serve the Moabite god. It was forbidden for them to intermarry. The people of Moab come from the incest of Lot with his daughters. **(Genesis 19:30-38).**

Nonetheless, Naomi and her husband turn to Moab during the famine, and Naomi's two sons marry Moabitess women: Orpah and Ruth. When the husband and sons die, Naomi decides to return to Bethlehem. Ruth asks Naomi to allow her to go with her, saying her land and her God will become her God. I believe this story reflects how merciful God is, how quick to want to forgive us of our backsliding. Naomi is returning to Bethlehem and calling herself "Mara" or "bitter." We can feel bitter where we have lost much, a husband and two sons, where we have suffered through destitute circumstances as Naomi did. We are instructed not to allow a root of bitterness to take hold in us, however, because it can destroy our fruit that we are presenting to the world, if you will. Keeping relationship with God prevents bitterness in all adverse circumstances. How wonderful to receive kindness when we have lost everything, when we have nothing. People respond to kindness, don't they? We can redeem people to God just by being kind to them. Our world is hungry for kindness.

That is what happens to Naomi and Ruth. Boaz hears of their plight and extends kindnesses to Ruth, and gives her purpose for her life. How wonderful when we, the church, extend love and kindness to our despairing world. Boaz represents how Jesus gives himself to redeem the church.

Our focus today is on Naomi, however. Let us also allow Naomi to represent something a moment. Let her represent some of us walking with the Lord. It appears that we cannot get what we need from God at times, from serving Him and walking in His ways; the trials and tests of Christians are confusing to us; we may ask why we are suffering when we are trying to serve the Lord. Sometimes, when the way becomes hard, we see Christians leave the church and return to the world, where they believe the lights are shining a little brighter. So, they leave church to follow after something they feel the world offers, something that looks like more provision. They begin to lose things that are important to them, however. They begin to lose their life and who they were in the Lord. Naomi loses a husband and two sons. Through this loss she decides to come home, back to what she was raised in, back to a faith in her God, back to a fellowship with those who believe as she believes. She brings a convert with her.

> "The Lord wants to bless you and redeem
> you and restore you to purpose."

Ruth has recognized something true in Naomi and she says she will serve her God. Faith begins to produce something. Naomi begins to have hope through what she sees is happening through Boaz, the kinsman-redeemer, and his kindness to Ruth, as he provides for both of them. She sends Ruth to claim a kinsman promise, and the redeemer/kinsman follows through to do his word. Naomi loses the bitterness as she remembers the promises of her God and has restoration of hope and faith brought back into her life.

Naomi is blessed in returning to the land of her God. So much so, that the child Boaz and Ruth have is nursed by Naomi and becomes the grandfather of King David. Ruth is one of four women mentioned in the lineage of Jesus Christ. What a blessing that Naomi has brought about and received unto herself by serving God, remembering His ways and following them, and bringing someone else under the umbrella of His protection. She had enough God in her even away from where He wanted her to be, that it made Ruth want to come to her God, instead of her following the god of the Moabites. How many Naomi's are trying to get back where they need to be in the Lord, and when they do, how many Ruth's will they be bringing into the church to know about the one true God of Israel? There is one true God and his name is Jesus. Much of the world is saying that there are many gods to serve and many ways to serve Him. Are we strong enough in the truth to see this error? Are we strong enough in God to bring the world to us, instead of them pulling us away from the one true God? I see people going into error a lot. Some of us may not feel very important in the kingdom of God, but if we have ever had any part in bringing someone to the knowledge of our Redeemer, we have done a great work. Naomi did a great work bringing Ruth back with her to the true God of Israel.

The Word of God says that those who save souls are wise. When we begin to win souls to the Lord, we will begin to recognize that we are walking into our God-ordained purpose. We belong to God and it is our job as Christians to reconcile people to God. The money you have given in offering that may have bought literature that went to a country across the sea that gave hope and understanding of our God to someone and that soul was saved--you will never know about that until you step into heaven. You were a part of that--perhaps that person became a great leader of other souls to the Truth--you were a part of that. Everything God puts in your heart to do for Him is important. Obey Him immediately in witnessing to others. Only in eternity will you understand the impact your obedience to God had in winning others to Him. Only in eternity will you understand the blessings you released to yourself and to others when you decided to forgive EVERYONE and extend mercy.

Whatever you have gone through or are going through--be it loss or betrayal--the Lord wants to bless you and redeem you and restore you to purpose. If you want to walk into your purpose, you first have to obey God in salvation, and then allow Him to work in and through you daily to serve Him in reaching others. You did not enter the kingdom of God to sit and eat at His table ALL of the time. You are to be laboring and harvesting for the kingdom of God. You are His servant as well as His beloved. If you would walk in His blessings, obey Him in extending mercy and forgiveness to all; obey Him in walking in love to all. If you get the love walk right, you do not have to worry about missing it in the law.

*Ways to Help Those in Need in Your
Church First, then Your Community*

Pray for them and with them.
Take them love offerings of food.
Give money if needed.
Invite them to lunch or dinner.
Encourage them by words and notes.
Promote them to others.
Give them a job.
Give rides to church or the store.
Study the Bible with them.
Give them resource books that speak
encouragement to their need.

Pray this aloud: Father, I ask that you would help me to glorify you in all I do. I ask you to help me to forgive immediately any and all injustices that will be performed against me in the future, or that have been committed against me in the past. If I need to apologize to someone to make something right, help me to do that to release them, as well as myself, from unforgiving feelings and attitudes. Thank you for your mercy and love and compassion. Help me to abide in You that the fruit I am producing is sweet. Let me look for ways to be kind and to show your love in action this week. Thinking good and pure and loving thoughts is wonderful, but let me show my love through actions purified and initiated by Your Spirit that those actions would be effectual in Your service. I really want to serve you and I really want to save others and bring them to a knowledge of Your love. Help me to do that. Don't let me hold anything in my heart that would prevent Your blessings from coming to me or prevent me from extending and sharing those blessings with others. Do this work in my heart now, Jesus! Melt me, refine and refashion me into a vessel of love and service for you my King. I love you so much. In Jesus name, Amen.

Week Three Worksheets

Overcoming Unforgiveness

"Therefore is the kingdom of heaven likened unto a certain king, which would take account of his servants. And when he had begun to reckon, one was brought unto him, which owed him ten thousand talents. But forasmuch as he had not to pay, his lord commanded him to be sold, and his wife, and children, and all that he had, and payment to be made. Matthew 18:23-25

Notes:

____

____

____

____

Define *forgiveness* in your own words:

____

____

How do you bind up your own blessings?

____

____

Who do you need to forgive in your life?

____

____

Who in your church needs your mercy and compassion?

____

____

How can you specifically ACT to help someone who needs help in your church?

____

____

F.A.I.T.H
Faithful Actions Initiated Through Him

"Love, joy, peace, patience, kindness, goodness, faithfulness, gentleness, self-control. Against such things there is no law." Galatians 5:22-23

Consider the following attributes of the fruit of the Spirit; if you are falling short in any area, try what is outlined by each one this week to refine your fruit.

Love: Smile at and speak kindly to everyone. Take time to call someone who has missed church.

Joy: This is our strength from God, so pray and praise this week until you get joy, and then spread it around.

Peace: It comes from staying in the secret place with the Father every time the trouble is trying to take first place. Just step back under the shadow of the Almighty, under His wings abiding. He is our hiding place. Pray.

Patience: No matter who flies in your face, practice keeping a calm face and a calm demeanor, and practice being proactive, rather than reactive to him or to her. Do not be in a rush, trust God, and wait on His answers. Allow people to interrupt you and give them your time and full attention, instead of looking put out with them.

Kindness: Do concrete actions to express this to others (bake a cake, open doors, write a note, give of yourself).

Goodness: Only God is good, so stay full of the Holy Ghost if you want this expressed. God in us is our only goodness.

Faithfulness: Obey the Spirit's promptings at once, discipline yourself in the study of The Word, in prayer daily, in witnessing, in assembling at church, in giving tithes and offerings.

Gentleness: Work on operating in a gentler, calmer way in your speech, in your actions.

Self-control: Keep your body under control, your appetites, your mannerisms, and your reactions to adverse circumstances.

This Week's Challenge

Examine the attributes of your fruit daily, and write in your journal those things you did to polish up your fruit this week. Keep writing down the specific things you pray for, and remember to write in when you get the answers. If you have been praying faithfully and specifically, I am sure you have already recorded dates of answered prayers.

Memory Verses

"I am the vine, ye are the branches: he that abideth in me, and I in him, the same bringeth forth much fruit: for without me ye can do nothing." John 15:5

"Therefore I say unto you, What things soever ye desire, when ye pray, believe that ye receive them, and ye shall have them. And when ye stand praying, forgive, if ye have aught against any: that your Father also which is in heaven may forgive you your trespasses. But if ye do not forgive, neither will your Father which is in heaven forgive your trespasses." Mark 11:24-25

WEEK FOUR

Overcoming Addictions

Have you ever seen such a world of addictiveness? Because we are in the flesh here on earth, there is not a person here who cannot fall to temptations of the flesh. Our flesh is in a continual battle with our spirit. Scripture says, "The spirit is willing, but the flesh is weak." It seems that many Christians are losing the battle with the flesh in our present world, but I know that Jesus said, "I have overcome the world." He set us free from the bondage of sin, but our flesh still has passions that we must learn to control to glorify God in our bodies as well as our spirits. Jesus said He would never leave us or forsake us and that He would send a Comforter to us. When we are weak, He is strong, and He has assured us that His grace is sufficient for each of us. We need to talk about addictions because we are not immune to being bound by addictions because we stepped into the Light. We are still in the flesh and we need to see what the Lord says to do about the battle we are in to keep our flesh subject to the Spirit. We also need to know how to help those without Jesus understand that He is bigger than their addiction. We can't help them until we are completely delivered from every addiction, however.

> **Pray this aloud: Father, you are an ever present help in time of trouble, and many times I am most troubled by this flesh in which I am housed. I am asking that your perfect will would be performed in my life, and I understand that one aspect of your perfect will for me is that I would subdue my own flesh and not allow my flesh to have the upper hand in making my decisions. I**

truly need to be Spirit led in every decision that I need to make each day. You came to set the captives free and to break every stronghold of Satan in my life. You have instructed in your Word how I may accomplish this overcoming in my flesh. I know that my flesh will even be fighting what your Spirit would be speaking to me in this lesson. I am taking authority over every spirit that wishes to exalt itself in my flesh and keep me from the knowledge of your Word concerning the overcoming of my flesh. Speak to me about any stronghold that I may be allowing in my life. Help me to identify the strongholds and to loose them by the power of your Word and Spirit. Only as I am completely set free from all bondage will I be able to effectively help others and pray for them to be loosed from their strongholds. Empower me with your spirit. Fill me with your agape love and bind every spirit of fear that would promote strongholds in me in Jesus name. Amen

**"I beseech ye therefore, brethren, by the mercies of God, that you present your bodies a living sacrifice, holy, acceptable unto God, which is your reasonable service. And be not conformed to this world, but be ye transformed by the renewing of your mind, that ye may prove what is that good and acceptable, and perfect will of God."
(Romans 12:1-2)** We really come to the Lord initially because we have discovered that all of the pleasures we pursued, and all of the things of the world that we have addicted ourselves to to fill up that emptiness within us--they just aren't enough to fulfill us. How many of you know that there is a place inside each heart that can only be filled with the presence of the Holy Spirit, anything else will not satisfy us? Until we get to the place of truly understanding that, however, we try to fill the empty place with stuff--food, drugs, alcohol, gambling, pursuit of riches, shopping until we drop, sex, pursuit of pleasures. We will sit in front of televisions, video games, computers, just mindless so that we can take our mind off the emptiness and loneliness that we so often feel in this world. Does Jesus want us to eliminate all of these things from our lives? Some of them that do damage to our bodies, yes. Some are areas where we must learn to be temperate. Webster's definition for *temperate* is "moderate in indulging the appetites." A definition for *addiction* is "to give oneself up to some strong habit." We

want to try to find a way to judge what needs to be given up to please God, and what requires temperance or moderation.

> "Jesus can help us with our addictions, but we have to lay them at His feet and not pick them up again."

Some of us are using addictions to fill that empty place in our spirit that we should be filling with God each day. We set things down when we initially come to the Lord, and we realized that He is what we need to fill that void. When we fail to stay in communication with Him and truly establish relationship with Him through prayer and study of His Word, however, we can find ourselves in trouble again, or sometimes we just do not understand the importance of moderation in all things, or maybe we are too ready to rely on the world's solutions to ease pain. Even as Christians, we turn to Him last at times when the problems arise. The flesh says it would be faster to take an aspirin for the headache, a Xanax for the depression, a Loritab for the pain, consume half a cake for the loneliness and the hurt, buy lottery tickets, take a trip to the casino, spend money we don't need to be spending in the hope of netting a windfall, shop until we drop, adding another top or skirt to a closet that is already overrun with clothing we never wear. Many are using those things for their emptiness and for pleasure. If they gave half of the time to God that they are giving to these things, we would have spiritual giants in the land. We forget that the Spirit will help us to deal with the symptoms of emptiness, and we forget that our bodies are not our own. He is waiting for us to call upon Him as we need strength to overcome every temptation of the flesh, and to break every stronghold holding us bound to addictions. The more we get control over our flesh, its appetites, and addictions, the more we can flow in the Spirit.

> "Do you know that the wicked will not inherit the kingdom of God? Do not be deceived, neither the sexually immoral nor idolators nor adulterers nor male prostitutes nor homosexual offenders nor thieves nor the greedy nor drunkards nor slanderers nor swindlers will inherit the kingdom of God. And that is what some of you were. But you were washed, you were sanctified, you were justified in the name of the Lord Jesus Christ and by the Spirit of our

> God. Everything is permissible for me--but everything is not beneficial. Everything is permissible for me--but I will not be mastered by anything." (II Corinthians 6:9-12)

> "What? Know ye not that your body is the temple of the Holy Ghost which is in you, which ye have of God, and ye are not your own?" (I Corinthians 6:19)

I believe this final scripture can keep us from arguing what is allowable and what is not. Someone smoking pot may argue that they are not doing anything worse than someone drinking coffee. The measuring place is damage to our body and allowing anything to master us. If what we are using our body to do, what we are filling up our time with, and what we are doing to please our flesh, has the upper hand over us or is doing damage to our body or altering our good judgment, we need to crucify that and take control. Our bodies are not our own. They have been bought with a price, and we are ambassadors of the Lord Jesus Christ to this world. All things are permissible as long as we can be temperate with them and not let them take the place of the time we should be spending with God, or let them be our escape from reality, when what we are truly needing is God's presence in our lives. We know that some things such as hard drugs are not something we can ever be temperate with and they are extremely destructive to our bodies, as well as our families, so they cannot be pleasing to God. They must be eliminated completely when we come to the Lord.

In modern day America, recession or not, we still live in one of the richest countries in the nations. All of the material benefits that we enjoy here have come at a spiritual price many times. Our money and material possessions get our attention when that attention should be on God and His will for our lives. We run here and there and enjoy one sinful pleasure after another trying to please our flesh. We have a momentary thrill that soon dissipates. Serving God and doing His will is the only true satisfaction in this life, but it takes a long time for some of us to come to this realization. If we understand the scriptures, we understand that we were delivered, justified, and sanctified when we were baptized into the Lord Jesus Christ.

We are not under law; there are things permissible to us, but not to the point ever of being mastered by them. We should always be conscious that our bodies are the temple of the Holy Ghost. Considering that should help us line up with God and take authority over anything that is trying to master us or become an addiction in our life. Coffee, pop, and tea are mildly addictive. I know ministers who have to set the iced tea down on occasion and fast from it just to make sure it isn't mastering them. We all know that these things are not sinful, but they are addictive enough to lead us from moderation to excess. I have had to lay down certain foods and drinks at times because they were controlling me instead of me controlling them. We go from these mild addictions to a myriad of more controlling addictions. Most of us are aware that there are times we try to feed our emotions by stuffing our faces. Food has gotten the upper hand with me on too many occasions, and I have to fast sweets or go on a complete fast for a couple of days to get a handle on **it. Ecclesiastes 10:17 says "Blessed art thou, O land, when---thy princes eat...for strength, and not for drunkenness!"** Because so many of us are walking around overweight and a testament to the abundant blessings of our land as well as gluttony (there, I said it), we avoid scriptures like this one. Very few times in the twenty five years I have served the Lord have I heard anyone chastising over the pulpit for gluttony, yet it is named clearly as a sin in the Bible. I have been guilty abundantly of this, I confess, and have worked hard the past several years to determine why I am eating and if it is too much. I am getting better, but the Lord still has a ways to take me. Let Him correct you in this area, too. This scripture says that we can be drunk on food. We can't eliminate food, though, as we can alcohol, can we? Living in the affluent society we live in, there is too much food around us tempting us to overindulge at times. We are to take the upper hand and figure out how to be moderate and keep ourselves from any temptations in this area. **Luke 21:34-36 says, "and take heed to yourselves, lest at any time your hearts be overcharged with surfeiting, and drunkenness, and cares of this life, and so that day come upon you unawares."** (Surfeiting means overindulgence in food or drink). If we want to take power over things quickly, we must pray and fast. God's help and strength is needed. Some of us have more willpower than others, but if we are dealing with food addictions, gambling addictions, alcohol or drug addictions, they are altering our will somewhat and we have to call on the power of God to be set free.

Many of us have people who we love with drug problems, and we have dealt continuously with the frustration of their addiction. Someone that I love has been bound for years by drugs. As a Christian, I have prayed and sent ministering angels to that person. I know that God has a day and an hour for the deliverance of that child, and I do not quit praying for him. The Lord showed me in a dream that he was bound; he could not get set free by himself, but he did want to be free. The drug has taken power over the drug addict because it is so highly addictive; so, if we do not continually pray for the deliverance of the drug addicts and those on alcohol, they may not ever get to the place of having the willpower on their own to be set free. The drug takes over their will, especially drugs such as meth. Hard drugs and alcohol addictions interfere with the will and judgment of men and women. Prayers for deliverance must continue until they are set free. It is too addictive. They need the Holy Ghost to set them free, and we are responsible to pray for that deliverance.

> **"Know ye not, that to whom ye yield yourselves servants to obey, his servants ye are to whom ye obey; whether of sin unto death, or of obedience unto righteousness?" (Romans 6:16)**

We want to obey the Lord and represent His righteousness before others, so it is important that we are moderate in all things before all people. Many people argue that anything that comes from plant life in Genesis would be given by the Lord for us to consume. They argue this for the use of caffeine, nicotine, and alcohol, which are all derived from plant life. Again, common sense and moderation must dictate. There are plants that would kill us dead in a few days if we consumed them. Sense dictates that this is not the use for which God intended them. If God made it, it is good to use (for something). God expects us to use wisdom and judgment. God wants us to be moderate in all things, and if we have learned that these substances cause us harm when abused, and we know that we cannot be moderate with them, we have to lay them aside. God says that a little bit of honey is okay in His Word, but Americans consume pounds of sugar every year, and this combined with the fast food fats added in are causing <u>tons</u> of trouble with our health.

We have to master our flesh through knowledge of God's Word, his Spirit reigning in us and giving us power over our flesh, and **we** have to say "**No**" to our flesh. We need to evaluate where we are in having control of our flesh. We need to overcome before we can help anyone else overcome. We can pray for one another, realizing that none of us are above any of these addictions except by the grace of God.

~ If we yield to God and not to our addictions, we have the key to mastery~

Our woman of faith this week was chosen because she had rather be at Jesus feet than anywhere else. Addictions will not master us if we spend our time with the Master.

Woman of Faith
Mary of Bethany

"Now it came to pass, as they went, that he entered into a certain village: and a certain woman named Martha received him into her house. And she had a sister called Mary, which also sat at Jesus' feet, and heard his word. But Martha was cumbered about much serving, and came to him, and said, Lord, dost thou not care that my sister hath left me to serve alone? Bid her therefore that she help me. And Jesus answered and said unto her, Martha, Martha, thou art careful and troubled about many things: but one thing is needful: and Mary hath chosen that good part, which shall not be taken away from her." (Luke 10:38-42)

Jesus commends this Mary several times in the scriptures. I see in these scriptures that she knows how to wait before the Lord, and learn at His feet, and another time, when Lazarus lay in the tomb dead, she is waiting quietly for the Lord, while Martha is running to Jesus and saying, "If you had been here, he would not have died." Martha is always concerned about and focused on the present circumstance or problem as she sees it. Mary, on the other hand, is sitting at Jesus feet and hearing His Word. We all start out at His feet when we come to the Lord, but then we get burdened up with cares and problems and we forget how we need to just set them at Jesus feet. Life is busy and we want things done when we want them done sometimes; we are like Martha, who Jesus must chastise because she asks him to make Mary help her with the serving. Jesus states that Mary hath chosen that good part, which shall not be taken away from her. Where else but at the feet of Jesus do we find our strength to overcome the problems, the burdens, and as we are speaking in this lesson, the addictions that want to try and master us? Are you like Mary or are you a Martha? Are you concentrating on the problem as Martha is, or are you focused on the problem solver? Maybe we need to switch our focus from the problem to Jesus. You know, most of us don't even know what moderate is until we have passed it. It is important to ask God to guide us in every aspect of our lifestyles. Run it by him if how you are spending your time, and what you are taking into the temple of the Holy Ghost, (your body), is okay with Him.

> **"But I keep under my body, and bring it into subjection, lest that by any means, when I have preached to others, I myself should be a castaway." (I Corinthians 9:27)**

A final thing I want to share with you is that even though we know how harmful many of the things we have discussed tonight can be to people, we should never change what the Bible actually says about things to try to eliminate addiction problems. God allows things sometimes in His Word, but with such a strong caution that as believers we know to refrain or to be moderate, but it is truly up to us to restrain our bodies, and to pray for strength from God as needed. I have actually heard preachers try to explain that the scriptures are referring to grape juice, where it says wine. It is obvious from the context of the passage they are speaking of wine which contains alcohol because they are speaking of effects it has on the person that grape juice would never have. Because wine or other forms of alcohol have been misused and have caused many problems for people and families because of being drunken to excess does not mean that we can personally eradicate what the Bible says about wine to fix the problem. The problem is ours in not heeding what the Bible says and remaining moderate. (Run scriptures in the Bible on *wine* from a Strong's Concordance sometime and see what the Word says and don't change it). I personally refrain from all alcoholic beverages because I do not want to even accidentally limit my judgment, and I know it would be a stumbling block to others to see me picking up wine downtown. The Word does tell us to refrain from doing things that may be a stumbling block to others. Wine fits in that category.

> **Pray this aloud: Heavenly Father, Help us to understand which addictions are so harmful to us that we must eliminate them completely from our lives. We pray tonight for our children and those who are outside who are bound by addictions to hard drugs or alcohol. We pray that You would break the bondage to these**

addictions in our communities. We also know that we are still in the flesh and must keep ourselves from allowing any addictions to rule us, no matter how minor they may seem to others. We must follow Your Word in seeing to it that nothing rules us, controls us, or keeps us away from time and service to You. Help us to turn to You more and more, Lord, to obtain guidance, comfort, and strength for our journey, relying on You in every moment when our flesh becomes weak and wants to reach for things that will lead us to be immoderate. Help us to keep our bodies in a way that glorifies You completely, and to ever keep in mind that we may need to refrain from some things that even You would allow if it would be a stumbling block to our brother and sister. We give You all praise, glory, and honor, In Jesus name. Amen.

WEEK FOUR WORKSHEETS

Overcoming Addictions

"I beseech ye therefore, brethren, by the mercies of God, that you present your bodies a living sacrifice, holy, acceptable unto God, which is your reasonable service. And be not conformed to this world, but be ye transformed by the renewing of your mind, that ye may prove what is that good and acceptable, and perfect will of God." (Romans 12:1-2)

Notes

____

____

____

____

"Do you know that the wicked will not inherit the kingdom of God? Do not be deceived, neither the sexually immoral nor idolators nor adulterers nor male prostitutes nor homosexual offenders nor thieves nor the greedy nor drunkards nor slanderers nor swindlers will inherit the kingdom of God. And that is what some of you were. But you were washed, you were sanctified, you were justified in the name of the Lord Jesus Christ and by the spirit of our God. <u>Everything is permissible for me--but everything is not beneficial. Everything is permissible for me--but I will not be mastered by anything.</u>" (II Corinthians 6:9-12)

"What? Know ye not that your body is the temple of the Holy Ghost which is in you, which ye have of God, and ye are not your own? (I Corinthians 6:19)

List here anything you are doing that while it may be permissible, it is not beneficial to your Christian walk; also, list any other thing that may be mastering you:

____

____

____

____

Anything that consumes so much of your time that you are neglecting giving God your time; anything that is causing conviction, yet you daily give yourself to it; anything pleasurable that you spend money on, feel you must have to get through your day, so much so that you would forfeit your tithes and offerings to God to be able to consume it on your lusts is an addiction. Since nothing is to come before your devotion to God, we can see how addictions become more than weights, and can become sins. Circle any of the things that may be mastering you in the list on the following page, rather than you mastering them. Some need to be eliminated totally from our lives, but others, such as food have to be mastered in a temperate fashion. If you are binge eating and throwing up food to keep your weight down, or if you are starving yourself to keep your weight down, you are addicted to food. We should be able to keep a realistic weight through moderation, making healthy eating choices, and fasting for spiritual purposes as the Lord directs (not to meet a worldly ideal weight that is unrealistic.)

Circle your problem areas

Beer	Tv	hard drugs	Pornography
Tea	videos	soda pop	(on computer or for women many
Alcohol	computers	cell phones	times in romance novels)/sex
Sugar	email/face book	shopping	
Coffee	texting	gambling	

Add anything else to list that you feel is an addiction for you that I have not listed here. Whatever you circled, (if you did), consider how much this week you are overdoing it, or if it is out and out sin, drop it at once, and pray for the Lord to strengthen you in this area.

NOTE: IF WE AREN'T GIVING IN TO ADDICTIONS OVER AND OVER WE WILL HAVE A VESSEL FOR THE LORD TO USE-- THAT IS THE GOAL OF THIS STUDY--OVERCOMING SO WE CAN IMPACT OUR WORLD FOR CHRIST!

Woman of Faith
Mary of Bethany

"Now it came to pass, as they went, that he entered into a certain village; and a certain woman named Martha received him into her house. And she had a sister called Mary, which also sat at Jesus' feet, and heard his word. But Martha was cumbered about much serving, and came to him, and said, Lord, dost thou not care that my sister hath left me to serve alone? Bid her therefore that she help me. And Jesus answered and said unto her, Martha, Martha, thou art careful and troubled about many things: But one thing is needful: and Mary hath chosen that good part, which shall not be taken away from her." (Luke 10:38-42)

Notes:

____

____

____

____

____

____

Martha

List here the things you are trying to take care of or overcome yourself.

____

____

____

____

____

____

____

Mary

List here the things you know you need to lay at Jesus feet.

____

____

____

____

____

____

____

This Week's Challenge

Lay aside every weight and sin because next week we are going to start examining the gifts of the spirit and we need to be ready to be strong in the Lord. To learn temperance, your challenge for this week is to address any addiction in your life as follows:

1) Honestly identify the addiction,

2) Pray and ask God to help you with it,

3) Add fasting to break the yoke (Isaiah 58:6),

4) Read God's Word in place of the time you would normally give to the addiction,

5) Deliberately break your routine and find a new place of service to God,

6) Keep prayer journaling.

Memory Verse

"I can do all things through Christ which strengtheneth me. (Phillipians 4:13)

WEEK FIVE

The Baptism of the Holy Ghost

You have read four lessons now on overcoming hindrances to your faith. I hope you have earnestly studied the scriptures and applied the challenges to this point, and feel yourself gaining some momentum over the negativity that you have faced and will continue to face as you do battle in your spiritual walk. God never meant for us to do this battle on our own power. Many Christians today are trying to do just that and are failing miserably, going around the same mountains, defeated time after time. We need the power that comes from receiving the baptism of the Holy Ghost. If you have never received this baptism, or if you have been told that you receive the Spirit of God when you believe and that is the same thing, I hope that you will open yourself to receive the Word of God in this lesson and be open to receive all of the gifts that God has for you, beginning with the baptism of the Holy Ghost. To receive His Spirit, the hindrances must be removed and we must be aligned with God's Word and willing to obey Him. He just needs a willing, repented, obedient heart.

God never wanted His church to be filled with weak, vacillating Christians. That is why He sent the Holy Ghost--His power working through us to witness and to deliver God's uncompromised Word to a lost world. That power we need gives us *sublime audacity*. As a teacher of literature, I love words. I particularly love the Word of God because it is powerful. The words *sublime audacity* are just fancy words that I particularly like because they basically mean "holy boldness." The Apostle Paul asked believers to pray for him that he would have this when he preached. The Apostle Peter and the other eleven apostles received this on the Day of Pentecost. Peter and the eleven never denied Jesus again after receiving the power and the boldness that came with the "gift of the Holy Ghost" received on that day. If you have not received the baptism of the Holy Ghost," please read this lesson carefully. We will be searching scriptures concerning what it truly means to be converted to live a Christ-like life, which is exactly what it means to be a Christian.

> **Pray this aloud: Father, I pray that Your will would be done in my life. I want to glorify You and be able to praise You in ways that are pleasing to You, sincerely, from the bottom of my heart. I want to be able to live a holy life before You and others and not go through each day feeling defeated in my walk with You. I thank You that You brought a way for us to reign in power here on earth as we are walking with You. I realize that I have much to learn about operating in Your ways and speaking and praying faith, but I am ready to learn. I am needing to be full of your Spirit and am asking You to fill me with the baptism of the Holy Ghost. Whatever I need to know to make my salvation sure and to become a powerful Christian witness to help others be saved, I am asking You to show it to me through your Word, by Your Spirit, and by Holy Ghost filled teachers and preachers. Help me to stand on the truth of Your Word even when what I am seeing and hearing from Your Word seems to contradict the traditions and beliefs I have learned from others in the world. Help me to always uphold and stand on Your Word as Truth. I wish to know Your ways and walk in them. Help me, Lord, to be unafraid as I walk with You. Help me to develop a deeper trust in You each day as I communicate with You in prayer and learn more about You through study of Your Word. In Jesus name. Amen.**

"And he said unto them, These are the words which I spake unto you, while I was yet with you, that all things must be fulfilled, which were written in the law of Moses, and in the prophets, and in the psalms, concerning me. Then opened he their understanding, that they might

> understand the scripture, And said unto them, Thus it is written, and thus it behooved Christ to suffer, and to rise from the dead the third day: And that repentance and remission of sins should be preached in his name among all nations, beginning at Jerusalem. And ye are witnesses of these things. And, behold, I send the promise of my Father upon you: but tarry ye in the city of Jerusalem, until ye be endued with power from on high." (Luke 24:45-49)

Jesus has taught these men three and one-half years; he has taught the crowds in parables at times, and then explained the parable aside to his disciples, but now, following his crucifixion and resurrection, he appears to them, showing them his hands and feet, and even eating in front of them to establish that he is alive, and at this point, he opens their understanding. It is time to understand fully His purpose. He instructs them to tarry in Jerusalem until they receive the promise and **POWER.** This is the group of men who have all failed and denied Jesus, the group of men who could not tarry one hour with Jesus in the garden of Gethsemane, but slept while Jesus agonized in prayer alone for strength to take on the cross and all of our sins. Now, however, the disciples have witnessed the resurrection; they have had their understanding opened, and following the ascension of Jesus, they do indeed tarry another ten days for the baptism of the Holy Ghost and the ensuing **POWER** that will cause these same men who failed Jesus to become the great leaders of the New Testament church, to become those who faced every kind of persecution, and even martyrdom, for the cause of Christ. Human effort can never do this; we all need the Holy Ghost to have the kind of **POWER** and boldness these disciples received.

Many churches today teach so many different things about the Holy Ghost. I do not even wish to list all of those, but I believe we can all agree on one thing here, and that is that God's Word is Truth, and that we can rightly divide that Truth, and be led by the Spirit of God to receive correct instruction on this matter.

Before we go into the counsel of the Lord, I would like to explain what the word *tarry* means, because if you have not received the Holy Ghost yet, *tarry* is what the Lord is wanting you to do to receive it, just like He required of that first 120 who "tarried" in the upper room. *Tarry* means more than "wait." It is the Greek word *kathize* that translates "sit" or "sit down." Throughout scriptures when the word *tarry* is used, it means: "to sit down and be taught, and teach, to have an intimate relationship with the Father, to sit down and count the cost, to sit down and worship, to sit down and pray with others. (This is what the disciples were to be doing until it was time to receive the Spirit). I want to take us through scriptures to show that Jesus meant each of us to receive the Holy Ghost as a part of our complete conversion experience. Christian believers are either not receiving this today because they haven't heard they can, because they are too busy with life to tarry, or because they are being disobedient to God in not giving him their heart completely.

Many preachers preach today and many Christians have believed that we are saved the moment we believe in Jesus. Some do not believe we even have to be baptized in water to be saved. Others say it is okay to baptize in the titles Father, Son, and Holy Ghost as Jesus commissioned in the book of Matthew, while others say the correct water baptism formula is to be baptized in the name of Jesus Christ as was done in the book of Acts. Many Christians today may say that they believe a believer can receive the baptism of the Holy Ghost if God chooses to give it to them; some say it isn't necessary for salvation. Since we know there is some dissension about when salvation happens and how it happens, shouldn't we make our calling and election sure by seeing what the whole Word of God says, rather than picking a few scriptures to stand on that are not correctly dividing the Word of Truth? So, how am I any different, you are probably asking yourself about now. Isn't that what I am going to do? Try to prove what I believe to you; am I not going to select the scriptures that prove what I believe about this to give to you? I can only let you judge. I will share some of my background here to totally open up where I am coming from in presuming to teach this: my experience: my testimony: most importantly, the Word of God. If you don't see it in the scriptures when you are through with this lesson, honestly searching the scriptures I am about to present, you may remain the same. If you want power in your Christian walk, however, if you want the Holy Ghost, you will need to "tarry" until you receive it. If God is trying to give us His greatest gift of Himself to help us lead an overcoming life here and have power to witness, how do you suppose He feels when we just nonchalantly say, "Well, if He wants me to have it, he'll give it to me." No, He wants you to see the value in it and want it more than eating, and then you will have it. He needs to know you will appreciate the gift and use it for His glory.

When does conversion take place? Were the disciples converted while they were walking with Jesus, seeing His miracles, and hearing all of His kingdom principles taught? Were they converted when He gave them power to heal the sick and cast out demons? Were they a converted lot who scattered and denied the Lord when He was taken by the soldiers? Was Peter converted when He receive the revelation from the Father that Jesus was the Christ? We have many believers today calling themselves Christians who do believe in Jesus, who do feel joy in their Christian walk, who have prayed a prayer of faith for people and seen them recover, who have even been in services and witnessed miracles. Those same believers can be moved on by the Spirit of God and led to know something or prompted to do something for others. I would like to show that they, as well as Peter and the disciples, are not what Jesus would consider to be converted YET at that point. I know I messed with all kinds of theology at this point, and there is no need in sending me scathing emails and letters about what I do and don't know. I confess, I am not a doctor of theology, but may I remind those of you who are that Jesus scolded those who were "ever learning and never coming to a knowledge of the truth." There is a truth to be found in the Word of God concerning conversion.

> **And the Lord said, "Simon, Simon, Satan hath desired to have you, that he may sift you as wheat: But I have prayed for thee, that thy faith fail not; and WHEN THOU ART CONVERTED, strengthen thy brethren."**
> **(Luke 22:31-32)**

Peter has been walking with Jesus, witnessing the miracles, performing some of His own by the power Jesus has given him, and I am sure that he even followed Jesus example to be baptized in water as John was teaching to do at this time; HE WAS A BELIEVER IF ANYONE WAS.

Yet, Jesus tells him, WHEN THOU ART CONVERTED, so we know that Jesus did not consider him converted at this point. ????? Don't leave me yet! Not only was Peter already laying hands on others and seeing them healed and demons cast out, but he also had received a word of knowledge at this point from the Father concerning who Jesus really was.

Many ministers on the radio, and I listen to several and appreciate so much some of their teaching on faith and walking this Christian walk, but we separate and go different directions when at the end of their broadcasts they ask anyone without Jesus who wants to be saved to say the sinner's prayer with them and now at that very moment they are saved. Believing in Jesus is a starting point to salvation, and I am not trying to make salvation hard, but I am not going to let Satan rob you of your full salvation experience because you have not heard ALL of the Word and divided it rightly. Do you know that **James 2:19** says that **"the devil believes and trembles"?** Is the devil going to be in heaven with us? **Mark 16:16** says, **"He that believeth and is baptized shall be saved."** "Shall" is a future tense verb and your salvation hinges on you obeying ALL that the Lord commands you to do to be saved.

What must we do then to be saved? That is the very question that many of the Jews asked Peter on the day of Pentecost, many who had betrayed Jesus and caused him to go to the cross of Calvary. **Acts 2:38** is what Peter gives them as the salvation message preached for the first time to the New Testament church, where following the 120 who had received the baptism of the Holy Ghost in the upper room on that day (including women and the mother of Jesus), now 3000 are added to the church as Peter tells them to: **"Be baptized, every one of you in the name of Jesus Christ for the remission of sins and ye shall receive the gift of the Holy Ghost."** This obeys the scripture in **Matthew 28** to **"go and baptize them in the NAME of the Father, Son, and Holy Ghost,"** because **Jesus name** is the **ONLY NAME** given whereby we might be saved. Peter did not mess up his first sermon.

I actually believe that many ministers who have baptized according to the Matthew formula believe that it would cause a big uproar in their church to tell everyone that they need to be baptized again in the name of Jesus, but when we get to heaven, the teachers and preachers of this gospel are going to stand accountable to God for what they taught, and as the truth of God's Word is revealed to us, we are responsible for it. Were there Christian believers who were rebaptized in the New Testament after they had already been baptized unto John's baptism? Yes. Why? Well, if the Apostle Paul showed up at your church and asked you if you had received the Holy Ghost since you believed and how had you been baptized, what would you tell him? Here is what the church at Ephesus told Paul, and what they heard from Paul and *immediately obeyed.*

"And it came to pass, that, while Apollos was at Corinth, Paul having passed through the upper coasts came to Ephesus: and finding certain disciples, He said unto them, Have ye received the Holy Ghost since ye believed? And they said unto him, We have not so much as heard whether there be any Holy Ghost. And he said unto them, Unto what then were ye baptized? And they said, Unto John's baptism. Then said Paul, John verily baptized with the baptism of repentance, saying unto the people, that they should believe on him which should come after him, that is on Christ Jesus. When they heard this, they were baptized in the NAME of the Lord Jesus. And when Paul had laid his hands upon them, the Holy Ghost came on them; and they spake with tongues, and prophesied. (Acts. 19:1-6.)

Maybe you are as these disciples; maybe you have never heard that you can receive the Holy Ghost and that you should be baptized in the name of Jesus Christ for the remission of your sins. Don't you think that we should be as the disciples at Ephesus, and when we have been shown the right way to be baptized of water and spirit by the Apostle Paul himself, that we should go about to obey and do it the right way? Or, do we wish to be like others that Paul taught and disputed within the temple: **"But when divers were hardened, and believed not, but spake evil of that way before the multitude, he departed from them, and separated the disciples, disputing daily in the school of one Tyrannus."** (Acts 19:9)

Do you know what sin is never forgiven? Jesus told us following the scribes accusing Him of casting out demons by the power of the prince of the devils. Jesus did not take lightly them saying that the power of the Holy Ghost was of the devil. He said, **"Verily I say unto you, All sins shall be forgiven unto the sons of men, and blasphemies wherewith soever they shall blaspheme: But he that shall blaspheme against the Holy Ghost hath never forgiveness, but is in danger of eternal damnation:"** **(Mark 3:28-29)** I wonder if we realize how serious it is to say that those churches who are teaching and receiving the baptism of the Holy Ghost are of the devil? What is Jesus saying about that? Do we want to let the Word of God stand as our counsel for the way Jesus wants things done, or do we want to hold to traditions and not rock the boat with our churches and families? Only you can decide what you will believe.

What did Jesus say we needed to do to enter the kingdom of God? There was a day when a ruler of the Jews, Nicodemus, came to Jesus by night, acknowledging that he knew Jesus was from God, and **"Jesus answered and said unto him, Verily, verily, I say unto thee, Except a man be born again, he cannot see the kingdom of God. Nicodemus**

saith unto him, How can a man be born when he is old? Can he enter the second time into his mother's womb, and be born? Jesus answered, Verily, verily, I say unto thee, Except a man be born of water and of the Spirit, he cannot enter into the kingdom of God." (John 3:3-8) Who was given the key to the kingdom, and what is a key for? Peter was given the key to the kingdom; it was Acts 2:38: that is how you get into the kingdom. The only key to open the door to the kingdom of God is found in **Acts 2:38**, where what was first given to Peter by Jesus is now given to the New Testament church by Peter (the one given the key) which tells us what Jesus meant when He said to Nicodemus that we must be born of "water" and "Spirit" to enter the kingdom of God. Is this making you mad? Let me share a bit of my testimony concerning this.

I was raised in a church where I heard about God the Father and where I heard about Jesus. I don't think I ever heard anything about the Holy Ghost. I was out of church for a number of years because I was looking for something that I did not find in that church (I did have an experience with repentance in that church and was baptized in the titles of God at age nine.) I lived in the world until I was 29 years old, and did not live well. I was hungry to know that God was real, and I visited some non-denominational churches, and listened to different teachers and preachers on television. I had remarried and my mother-in-law was a Pentecostal believer and when she shared her testimony with me, she stated that her sister had come from a brush arbor meeting when they were kids, and said, "Norma, did you know that God is real?" This struck a chord in me because I had been looking in the heavens and telling God that He was going to have to show me if He was real. He did. I started attending this church, and I had never before sat under anointed preaching like this before. I wept through the entire service about three times before I went to the altar. The assistant pastor was quick (just like the disciples) to get to me and expound the Word of God and show me Jesus name baptism and the infilling of the Holy Ghost. I was <u>rebaptized</u> in Jesus name, and as I have stated earlier in these lessons, it was about three years before I received the Holy Ghost, not because God wants to make it hard for us, but because I was holding onto unforgiveness in my heart. His Spirit doesn't dwell in an unforgiving heart. God is love and when He fills us with the Holy Ghost, we have the love of God shed abroad in our hearts. When we are baptized in Jesus name, our sins are remitted, (they are put as far away from us as the east is from the west the Word of God says.) God may wait and try our hearts before He fills us with the Holy Ghost. How badly do you want to be filled? I prayed about every service at the altar for three years. I saw it was real and I fought for it. Jacob wrestled with the angel of the Lord for his blessing. Scripture tells us the "violent take it by force." When you see it in the Word, fight for it; don't be robbed of God's blessings through a lazy attitude and not appreciating the value of your birthright as Esau.

The baptism of the Holy Ghost is first poured out on the 120 in the upper room, then it is poured out on the Jews. To see when it is given to the Gentiles, we need to look at **Acts 10.** I hope that you will turn there and read all of that chapter. I will only address the actual preaching of Peter to Cornelius (the first Gentile, along with his family, to receive the baptism of the Holy Ghost). They **heard** them receive it, they did not just believe by faith it was received.

"While Peter yet spake these words, the Holy Ghost fell on all them which heard the word. And they of the circumcision which believed were astonished, as many as came with Peter, because that on the Gentiles also was poured out the gift of the Holy Ghost. For they heard them speak with tongues, and magnify God. Then answered Peter, Can any man forbid water, that these should not be baptized, which have received the Holy Ghost as well as we? And he commanded them to be baptized in the name of the Lord. Then prayed they him to tarry certain days." (Acts 10:44-48)

WEEK FIVE WORKSHEETS

The Baptism of the Holy Ghost

Why is this lesson in this place in this Bible study? If you believe in Jesus Christ and are in earnest enough to grow as His disciple, so earnest that besides studying your Bible and going to church to hear the preached Word, you are studying a Bible study to help you grow so you can minister to others, I believe you need to know that it is the Holy Ghost power of God that will enable you to do the ministry to others that you want to do. He will draw people to Him through you, if you will be filled with His Spirit, and if you already have been, if you will stay full of His Spirit.

Consider the following questions.

Have you received the Holy Ghost with evidence of speaking in tongues?

____

____

Have you always believed that as soon as you confess Jesus as your Lord you are saved, and you have perhaps been taught that anything else is not of grace?

____

____

Do you want all that God has for you to enable you to be a bold and powerful witness?

____

____

Are you willing to ask God daily to baptize you with His Spirit until you receive it?

____

____

Are you arguing with the scriptures I have presented to you?

____

____

Why?

____

____

____

____

If you see your need to be rebaptized in the name of Jesus Christ and to be filled with the baptism of the Holy Ghost, please find an apostolic church that teaches this and obey what you have seen in the Word of God.

Describe here your present experience with the Lord regarding your salvation process:

____

____

____

____

____

We will be learning that we are told in the scriptures to stay full of the Spirit, to pray in the Spirit, to ask for spiritual gifts, and to keep our gifts stirred up. Staying full of God and making sure He is abiding in us and we are abiding in Him is our secret to having His POWER working in us and through us. We can't be without it and overcome. We can't be without it and be bold witnesses. We can't be without it.

This Week's Challenge

Look at the following scriptures in any version of the Bible you enjoy studying this week. Pray for the baptism of the Holy Ghost if you have not yet received it.

Acts 1:8
Acts 9:11-18
Acts 2:36
Acts Chapter 10
Acts 2:37-39
Acts 19:2-6

Memory Verse

"Then Peter said unto them, Repent, and be baptized, every one of you in the name of Jesus Christ for the remission of sins and ye shall receive the gift of the Holy Ghost." Acts 2:38

F.A.I.T.H.
Faithful Actions Initiated (Through Him)

When we have allowed Him to take up residence in us through the baptism of the Holy Ghost, it is now Him that is doing the work through us, and not us trying to get it done. Now our faithful actions will have a purpose that comes through Him and His will.

WEEK SIX

Gifts of the Spirit

The Lord wants a unified church. We are the actual body of Christ here on this earth today, and the way we work as a unified body is to be led by a central force, the way the brain is the central force of our body; it gets us to walk without tripping ourselves, or we can raise a fork and hit our mouth instead of taking out our eyeball, or we can lay down when that is what is intended instead of part of our body wanting to stand, while the other part tries to lay down. A brain is important, isn't it, for our physical body to coordinate and function together to serve the purpose we need it to serve at any given moment? The only way the church can be a unified body is to hear the voice of God, be led by His Spirit, and learn to acknowledge and respect the offices and gifts He has placed in His body, the church: that's us. The other thing we need to understand is that we owe Jesus our bodies individually to work through, to do our part in the corporate body, which is the church. When one member isn't working, the rest of the body isn't operating perfectly. We need to understand the difference between talents and gifts of the Spirit. We need to understand that God tells all of us to covet spiritual gifts, and to pray for the gift of prophesy, and the purpose is this: to edify His church body, to help us grow in the knowledge of who He is, to help us understand His Word, to help us know how to love and care for one another, to help us to minister, and most importantly, to bring Him glory. The gifts of the Spirit are not to glorify one individual; even though some of the gifts are more visible than others, no one is to be held higher than another. We are all using the gifts to corporately grow as a church body giving honor to Jesus. The gifts are to edify the church. To be effective, the gift must be directed by the Holy Spirit. I believe we all were born with a certain plan for our lives and received talents or abilities that were gene given, or related to our flesh, but the gifts of the Spirit are something different; they are bestowed upon us as God wills when we are born again spiritually. It is important to receive the baptism of the Holy Ghost so these gifts can operate by His Spirit and not be us trying to operate a gift in our own flesh. If you have not received the baptism of the Holy Ghost, keep growing in the Word, and be quick to obey and serve the Lord, and He will fill you as you continue to seek Him.

> **Pray this aloud: Father, I know you are a great God and that you want me to be able to share my knowledge of your grace and atonement with others. Help me to lay aside the weights, the hindrances, and any secret sins so I am able to walk more confidently as a Christian. Give me a sublime audacity to witness. Empower me with the gifts of the Spirit you wish me to use to help edify my brothers and sisters in the church, and to reach those without your salvation. I pray for the gift of prophecy that I might have the supernatural ability to speak Your Word to the right person at the right time. I pray that you would baptize me with your Spirit, with your love, and with your mercy that it would be your perfect love in me that I am giving to my broken world. I know that you are "able to do abundantly above all I can think or ask according to this power _working in me_ and _through me_. Thank you, Jesus. Amen.**

"He who descended is the one who ascended, that He might fill all things and he gave the apostles, the prophets, the evangelists, the shepherds and teachers, to equip the saints for the work of ministry for building up the body of Christ, till we all come in the unity of the faith, and of the knowledge of the Son of God, unto a perfect man, unto the measure of the stature of the fullness of Christ..." (Ephesians 4:10-13)

I want to briefly explain the five-fold ministry before we attend to other gifts. The five fold ministry is a gift to the church to prepare the saints for their work of ministry in building up the body of Christ. If you attend a traditional church, you may just be considering three of the five fold ministries within your churches, but I believe that there is still a five-fold ministry God means to be in the churches helping to grow up the body of Christ. Some may argue that there are not apostles today, but I believe that part of the ministry is done by our missionaries; they may not be calling themselves apostles, but they are introducing doctrine and church discipline for the first time in new areas, so I believe that fulfills the role of "apostles." Some of you may be uncomfortable with the term "prophet," and while some today may try and misuse this ministry to try and take advantage of a church, a true prophet of God in today's church can be a separate ministry than that of pastor or evangelist with a specific call to proclaim things from God's Word. The pastor is also fulfilling this gift as he discerns through the anointing of God and tells forth the things of God. An evangelist will be very much focused on the Gospel of Jesus Christ and presenting it to the lost. A pastor loves his flock and cares for the needs of the church family, preparing sermons to encourage them, being there when there are times of illness or death. A teacher's gifting is the ability to instruct and help others apply the Word of God practically in their daily lives. Some of the gifts in the five fold ministry may overlap. A pastor may be able to move in the gifting of a prophet or a teacher as needed.

I think we all believe it is the pastor's job to do all of the ministering sometimes, but the church body is supposed to receive and recognize their spiritual gifts and we are all supposed to be performing ministry as we are called. Not all of us will preach, teach, or evangelize, but each of us has been given one or more spiritual gifts that we must identify so that we are doing our part to edify the body of Christ. In the Old Testament they had prophets who spoke as the oracle of God when the Holy Ghost moved on them. They had priests who would offer the sacrifice to atone for their sins. Jesus changed everything and He brought a new way of doing things that began with Him atoning for our sins and ascending to heaven, so that now the Holy Ghost could be given. The Holy Ghost makes us all kings and priests because now God chooses to speak directly to us and lead us by His Spirit, (this is how privileged we are to receive the baptism of the Holy Ghost--only prophets in the Old Testament could experience what we now all can experience as sons and daughters of God). In the Old Testament, God moved on the prophets to speak through them; today He uses us to expand His church by speaking through us and using us as He wills; first, by using the five-fold ministry to train us, and then imparting spiritual gifts to each of us so that we can minister in the fashion He chooses for us to minister. He gives these gifts to help the church grow up and to unify us as one body in Him. A church that utilizes the five-fold ministry gifts and a church that will find and use their spiritual gifts is a unified church, and one that is grown up enough to be effective in the proclaiming of the gospel to others. God never meant for our five-fold ministry to be our entertainment, while the rest of us sit on the pew as spectators doing nothing. God has a purpose and direction for each of us, and we need to inquire of Him to find that purpose.

What is the purpose for the gifts? I have already said they are to edify the church, to bring unity in the church, and to grow up the church. If nonbelievers come into church, there are spiritual gifts of tongues and interpretation, healings, and miracles that can help them to believe if in operation, **IF the saints will be open to God using them in these gifts. Hebrews 2:4** states, **"God also bearing them witness, both with signs and wonders, and with divers miracles, and gifts of the Holy Ghost, according to his own will."** I **Corinthians 14:3-5 states, "But he that prophesieth speaketh unto men to edification, and exhortation, and comfort. He speaking in an unknown tongue edifieth himself; but he that prophesieth edifieth the church… that the church may receive edifying."** We see another important aspect of the gifts of the Spirit: to edify, exhort, to comfort.

Finally, the gifts are to establish each of us in our ministry to the rest of the body of Christ. **Romans 1:11** says, **"For I long to see you, that I may impart unto you some spiritual gift, to the end ye may be established."** I do not really witness much laying on of hands in our churches to impart gifts other than the receiving of the Holy Ghost, but the Apostle Paul laid hands on disciples and imparted "gifts" to them, so I certainly don't see how it would be out of order for our Holy Ghost ministers to lay hands on the disciples under their teaching and impart spiritual gifts to them as the Holy Ghost tells them to do so.

What are the gifts that the church should receive? We need to read all of **I Corinthians 12, 13, and 14** in this lesson, for the purpose of this week's lesson and as a foundation for a later teaching on women's roles in the church. These chapters are written to the church in Corinth, and Paul is teaching and chastising a church: he is instructing in what the spiritual gifts are, bringing order to the church in their use of the gifts, and instructing that love is the most important factor in our church; even so, he still instructs us to "desire" the spiritual gifts. It would seem that perhaps some were getting lifted up and out of order in the use of their gifts.

Paul explains the gifts, and explains that we are all baptized into one body:

Now concerning spiritual gifts, brethren, I would not have you ignorant. Ye know that ye were Gentiles, carried away unto these dumb idols, even as ye were led. Wherefore, I give you to understand, that no man speaking by the Spirit of God calleth Jesus accursed: and that no man can say that Jesus is the Lord, but by the Holy Ghost. Now there are diversities of gifts, but the same Spirit. And there are differences of administrations, but the same Lord. And there are diversities of operations, but it is the same God which worketh all in all. But the manifestation of the Spirit is given to every man to profit withal. For to one is given by the Spirit the word of wisdom; to another the word of knowledge by the same Spirit; To another faith by the same Spirit; to another the gifts of healing by the same Spirit; To another the working of miracles; to another prophecy; to another discerning of spirits; to another divers kinds of tongues; to another the interpretation of tongues: But all these worketh that one and the selfsame Spirit, dividing to every man severally as he will.

For as the body is one, and hath many members, and all the members of that one body, being many, are one body: so also is Christ. For by one Spirit are we all baptized into one body, whether we be Jews or Gentiles, whether we be bond or free; and have been all made to drink into one Spirit. For the body is not one member, but many. If the foot shall say, Because I am not the hand, I am not of the body; is it therefore not of the body?

And if the ear shall say, Because I am not the eye, I am not of the body; is it therefore not of the body? If the whole body were an eye, where were the hearing? If the whole were hearing, where were the smelling? But now hath God set the members every one of them in the body, as it hath pleased him. And if they were all one member, where were the body? But now are they many members, yet but one body. And the eye cannot say unto the hand, I have no need of thee: nor again the head to the feet, I have no need of you. Nay, much more those members of the body, which seem to be more feeble, are necessary:

And those members of the body, which we think to be less honorable, upon these we bestow more abundant honour; and our uncomely parts have more abundant comeliness. For our comely parts have no need: but God hath tempered the body together, having given more abundant honour to that part which lacked: That there should be no schism in the body; but that the members should have the same care one for another. And whether one member suffer, all the members suffer with it; or one member be honored, all the members rejoice with it. Now ye are the body of Christ, and members in particular. And God hath set some in the church, first apostles, secondarily prophets, thirdly teachers, after that miracles, then gifts of healings, helps, governments, diversities of tongues. Are all apostles? are all prophets? Are all teachers? Are all workers of miracles? Have all the gifts of healing? Do all speak with tongues? Do all interpret? But covet earnestly the best gifts: and yet show I unto you a more excellent way. Though I speak with the tongues of men and of angels, and have not charity, I am become as sounding brass, or a tinkling cymbal. And though I have the gift of prophecy, and understand all mysteries, and all knowledge; and though I have all faith, so that I could remove mountains, and have not charity, I am nothing. And though I bestow all my goods to feed the poor, and though I give my body to be burned, and have not charity, it profited me nothing. Charity suffereth long, and is kind; charity envieth not; charity vaunted not itself, is not puffed up, Doth not behave itself unseemly, seeketh not her own, is not easily provoked, thinketh no evil; Rejoiceth not in iniquity, but rejoiceth in the truth; Beareth all things, believeth all things, hopeth all things, endureth all things. Charity never faileth: but whether there be prophecies, they shall fail; whether there be tongues, they shall cease; whether there be knowledge, it shall vanish away. For we know in part, and we prophesy in part. But when that which is perfect is come, then that which is in part shall be done away. When I was a child, I spake as a child, I understood as a child, I thought as a child: but when I became a man, I put away childish things. For now we see through a glass, darkly; but then face to face: now I know in part; but then shall I know even as also I am known. And now abideth faith, hope, charity, these three;

but the greatest of these is charity. Follow after charity, and desire spiritual gifts, but rather that ye may prophesy. For he that speaketh in an unknown tongue speaketh not unto men, but unto God: for no man understand him; howbeit in the spirit he speaketh mysteries. But he that prophesieth speaketh unto men to edification, and exhortation, and comfort. He that speaketh in an unknown tongue edifieth himself; but he that prophesieth edifieth the church. I would that ye all spake with tongues, but rather that ye prophesied: for greater is he that prophesieth than he that speaketh with tongues, except he interpret, that the church may receive edifying. Now, brethren, if I come unto you speaking with tongues, what shall I profit you, except I shall speak to you either by revelation, or by knowledge, or by prophesying, or by doctrine? And even things without life giving sound, whether pipe or harp, except they give a distinction in the sounds, how shall it be known what is piped or harped? For if the trumpet give an uncertain sound, who shall prepare himself to the battle? So likewise ye, except ye utter by the tongue words easy to be understood, how shall it be know what is spoken? For ye shall speak into the air. There are, it may be, so many kinds of voices in the world, and none of them is without signification. Therefore if I know not the meaning of the voice, I shall be unto him that speaketh a barbarian, and he that speaketh shall be a barbarian unto me. Even so ye, forasmuch as ye are zealous of spiritual gifts, seek that ye may excel to the edifying of the church. Wherefore let him that speaketh in an unknown tongue pray that he may interpret. For if I pray in an unknown tongue, my spirit prayeth, but my understanding is unfruitful. What is it then? I will pray with the spirit, and I will pray with the understanding also: I will sing with the spirit, and I will sing with the understanding also. Else when thou shalt bless with the spirit, how shall he that occupieth the room of the unlearned say Amen at the giving of thanks, seeing he understandeth not what thou sayest? For thou verily givest thanks well, but the other is not edified. I thank my God, I speak with tongues more than ye all: Yet in the church I had rather speak five words with my understanding, that by my voice I might teach others also, than ten thousand words in an unknown tongue. Brethren, be not children in understanding:

howbeit in malice be ye children, but in understanding be men. In the law it is written, With men of other tongues and other lips will I speak unto this people; and yet for all that will they not hear me, saith the Lord. Wherefore tongues are for a sign, not to them that believe, but to them that believe not: but prophesying serveth not for them that believe not, but for them which believe. If therefore the whole church be come together into one place, and all speak with tongues, and there come in those that are unlearned, or unbelievers, will they not say that ye are mad? But if all prophesy, and there come in one that believeth not, or one unlearned, or unbelievers he is convinced of all, he is judged of all: And thus are the secrets of his heart made manifest; and so falling down on his face he will worship God, and report that God is in you of a truth. How is it then, brethren? When ye come together, every one of you hath a psalm, hath a doctrine, hath a tongue, hath a revelation, hath an interpretation. Let all things be done unto edifying. If any man speak in an unknown tongue, let it be by two, or at the most by three, and that by course; and let one interpret. But if there be no interpreter, let him keep silence in the church; and let him speak to himself, and to God. Let the prophets speak two or three, and let the other judge. If any thing be revealed to another that sitteth by, let the first hold his peace. For ye may all prophesy one by one, that all may learn, and all may be comforted. And the spirits of the prophets are subject to the prophets. For God is not the author of confusion, but of peace, as in all churches of the saints. Let your women keep silence in the churches; for it is not permitted unto them to speak; but they are commanded to be under obedience, as also saith the law. And if they will learn anything, let them ask their husbands at home: for it is a shame for women to speak in the church. What? came the word of God out from you? Or came it unto you only? If any man think himself to be a prophet, or spiritual, let him acknowledge that the things that I write unto you are the commandments of the Lord. But if any man be ignorant, let him be ignorant. Wherefore, brethren, covet to prophesy, and forbid not to speak with tongues. Let all things be done decently and in order. (I Corinthians Chapters 12, 13, and 14.)

Paul goes on in these three chapters to caution that while these gifts are all great and to be desired, they are nothing if they are not operated through love. We are to desire these gifts to help one another grow in the church, not to make ourselves seem more spiritual than others. He gives guidelines in the final chapter for the use and the order of gifts to be used in the church. Let's examine the different gifts and their uses. (We will deal in another lesson about women's roles in the church). Let's use these scriptures for a foundation to begin to break down the gifts and explain what they are.

First, **the gift of wisdom**. We are instructed in James 1:5-8 to pray for wisdom and that the Lord will give it to us. Sometimes, you may find yourself out of your league about a situation you have to deal with, how to minister to someone's need, or even how to pray with someone, and you will get a supernatural inspiration from the Lord, sometimes even a scripture to share, or you will say and pray just the right thing for them and you know it is not from your natural understanding. This is a gift of wisdom in operation. God gave Simon Peter the spiritual insight to understand who Jesus was, and he stood up and proclaimed that Jesus was the Christ in Matthew 16:16-18

Second, **the gift of knowledge**. In John 4:17-18 Jesus demonstrates a gift of knowledge concerning a woman he is visiting with that has had five husbands, and is now living with a man. She has told Jesus she has no husband, but He sees there is more to it--the number of husbands and the living with a man. This is a gift of knowledge.

Once, when I was going through a particularly difficult situation, and there were people who knew what I was going through, they would say to me, "You just look so at peace." I may have looked on the outside like I was staying in peace, but my mind was telling me that "You are going to lose your mind. You are going to have a nervous breakdown." God sent someone by to invite me to a revival, and when I went, I had invited a couple of women to go with me. I was sort of hoping the service wouldn't get too "pentecostal" and rambunctious, but no such luck. The young evangelist is ministering and suddenly walks back toward me, steps into the pew in front of me, looks at me and says, "God told me to tell you that you are not going crazy and you are not going to have a nervous breakdown." He placed his hand on my forehead and the power of God hit me and I went to my knees wailing. This was not what I had intended for my dear visitors to witness, but I went home knowing that my God knew all about where I was and He wasn't putting up with me going into a pity party just because the trials of life were intense. My fourteen-year-old son who was rather indignant normally about any manifestations of the Spirit even said on the way home that night that "You have needed that for a while."

Maybe what I just shared with you seems like "too much" to you. If you have been raised in a traditional church, I understand. I was raised in a traditional church, too, but I would not trade any of what I have experienced in walking more closely with the Lord in the power of Pentecost the past 25 years. When **God** shares knowledge about you with someone, it is never to hurt you, but always to heal you and He will share it with a mature person who loves you and is operating in God's spirit. Don't be afraid of these gifts. Remember that they are to build the church.

Allow me to share one other instance of the gift of knowledge from personal testimony. I was going through this very hard thing, still related to the preceding story. I was reading my Bible in bed one night, and reading the part about receiving "beauty for ashes." I stopped reading and said to God, "This is what I need. I feel like my entire past is burned up and I don't even want to start all over again. I need this "beauty for ashes. I don't even understand it, but I need it."

I go to another revival. This preacher is preaching my life that night. I am sitting on the back pew (you might as well announce you are practically backslid sitting back there), feeling no joy. At the end of the service, everyone is up at the altar praising the Lord (a very demonstrative church), and I am just sitting alone on the back pew with my head down. The minister says, "Ma'am, I don't want to embarrass you, but would you please come and let my wife pray for you? I would like for her to intercede for you." I go obediently to the front and his wife wraps her arms around me and starts praying in the Holy Ghost. Before long I was breaking out in dance and laughing, just feeling the joy. When things settle down and a very sweet spirit of the Lord is just lingering, (no one wants to leave when it is like that), the preacher steps down to me (a preacher from another state who doesn't know me from Adam, and no one knows what I said that night in my bed except God) and he says in my ear only, "The Lord has seen the fiery trial of your faith and He is bringing you beauty for ashes." That is a gift of knowledge and I was strengthened that night as God sent a word of knowledge to a minister who encouraged and strengthened me. God has been true to His Word and sent me beauty for ashes. I love living for God, and I appreciate daily the deliverance from my former mess of a life. The gifts help.

Third, is **the gift of faith.** We have all been given a measure of faith and we know that without faith it is impossible to please God. A gift of faith, however, is the ability to believe God for the supernatural in incredible situations. David believing to go against Goliath is an example of supernatural faith. When we hit trials and God gives us a gift of faith to persevere to see things through until the turnaround, not doubting, is a gift of faith. Faith comes in two ways: **Romans 10:17** says, **"So then faith comes by hearing, and hearing by the word of God."** We gain faith through hearing the preached Word of God. We gain faith by taking steps of faith, trusting God even more as we mature. **James 1:3** says, **"You know that the testing of your faith develops perseverance."** This is maturity in the faith. There have been times I have prayed for others trying to have faith, and there have been times I have prayed for others with "the gift of faith." The gift made a difference.

Fourth, **gifts of healing**. Someone may operate in the gifts of healing more than another, but God operates this gift as He wills. We all pray and believe, and leave the results to him. There are people who may claim to be faith healers today, but we need to be careful because there are counterfeits to this gift. There is the real gift of healing from God, however, and most of us have benefited as a result of these gifts in our own bodies. I remember an evangelist laying hands on me at the altar one time, and I know that the Lord gave him a gift of knowledge and a gift of healing to minister to me. I did not ask for prayer. I was just worshipping at the altar. Every joint in my body was hurting terribly. I felt like I was under attack. This evangelist came and laid hands on me, and commanded the pain to leave all of my joints. He spoke with authority and conviction because he was operating in those gifts. I was healed immediately. Jesus not only atoned for our sins at Calvary, but He paid for our healing with 39 stripes on His back. I recently heard someone say that the medical community has classified diseases into 39 broad categories. I thought that was interesting when I heard it. Jesus paid for all of those. If we have sicknesses in our body, we have instructions in the Word what to do. **James 5:14-15** says, **"Is any one of you sick? He should call the elders of the church to pray over him and anoint him with oil in the name of the Lord. And the prayer offered in faith will make the sick person well; the Lord will raise him up. If he has sinned, he will be forgiven."** Don't fail to go to the elders first for prayer. **IF** we will obey what the Word says to do, believing, we will receive our healings.

Fifth, is **the gift of miracles**. Miracles are not given to build the believers faith, but to convince the unbeliever of the power of God. The Bible says that miracles "follow them that believe." We do not have to have a special miracle service. They simply follow those who believe. Sometimes, a healing is a miracle. It happens instantaneously rather than as a speeded-up recovery. Miracles would include raising the dead to life, casting out demons, miraculous healings of the lame, deaf, blind. These did not stop with Jesus. Many miracles are being seen in today's churches where the Holy Ghost is allowed to work. You can get on the Internet and look up missionary stories in third world countries and see many miracles being performed as Jesus is giving these manifestations to help non-believers come to a saving knowledge of Him. The purpose of these gifts is not to make a big side-show for us or for Jesus. They are given to bring people into church and to help grow them up to become workers in the ministry to others also.

Sixth, **the gift of prophesy.** In chapter 14 of I Corinthians, we read that Paul tells us we should desire spiritual gifts, and particularly this gift of prophecy, because it is this gift that brings unity to the church. This gift tells who God is, what He has done, and what He plans on doing. We should desire this so we can speak a word to someone that is timely and gives them direction. It is not for preachers and prophets only. For example, I know of an instance where a preacher felt a direction for a service, but wasn't sure, so he told God that he would go ahead with it if He confirmed that word during the service before He preached, and God used one of the saints to speak and confirm that word during a time of testimony. That is an example of a gift of prophecy used through the saint as well as the pastor.

Seventh, **the gift of distinguishing of spirits.** In Acts chapter 16, the Apostle Paul has a woman diviner or fortune teller following Him, proclaiming him and the others to be servants of the Most High God. While this is true, having someone who was speaking by an evil spirit proclaim this was not good. Paul recognized the spirit by discernment and told it to come out of the woman. We all need to pray for discernment of spirits, because the Word of God tells us that there are false prophets, and even Satan is transforming himself into an angel of light in these last days. Without discernment, we can have confusion. God is not the author of confusion, and we want him to lead us to discern wrong spirits. He may give this gift more to the five-fold ministry to recognize.

Eighth, **the gift of tongues.** There is division and confusion about this gift. The initial evidence of tongues that you may speak when you receive the Holy Ghost is one thing; some may have a gift to speak with tongues more than others as a devotional tongue where they are speaking to God, and then there is the tongues given that is spoken out during a service to confirm or expand what is being said by the minister in a service, and this use should always be followed with an interpretation. When you speak in tongues, you are not speaking gibberish that someone taught you to speak. You are speaking with faith as the spirit of God gives you utterance. You operate the gift, but God is giving you fluency in a language that you have never learned. It is a real language. It is a sign to unbelievers and it is a building up of the church when interpretation follows it, and a building up of the believer when they are praying in the Spirit, even without interpretation, privately. If we speak in tongues, we should be praying that the Lord would help us to interpret, so that more than our spirit is fruitful, but also our minds.

Ninth, **interpretation of tongues**. This is the ability of a believer to hear a message in a language you have never learned and interpret it for others to understand. I have witnessed this interpretation a number of times, and it is always edifying to the church. It always blesses the church and instructs, chastises, or comforts. Saints know the Lord is present and it is a real blessing.

We are to desire all of the gifts of the Spirit that the Lord will give us, but we are not to strive or divide over them. God gives them severally as He wills for His purpose. The same Spirit works the gifts, like the brain moves our bodies. We are all a part of the body, remember, but we are all different members, made wonderfully by God, given special individual talents and then blessed with spiritual gifts, so that we can support and build each other up. We all need to be praying for God to help us understand our gifts, give us gifts, help us to use them, and begin to step out in faith in any areas we feel that the Lord is leading us to find our gifts. Sometimes, others may recognize a gift working in us that we are simply taking no notice of, so we should all be mindful to help each other recognize gifts. We are obviously not all called to the five-fold ministry. We are all called to be used in the gift or gifts that God gives to us and to operate in love at all times. Paul shows us this in **I Corinthians 12:31,** where he says, **"But eagerly desire the greater gifts. And now I will show you the most excellent way."** That way is love. Many people use this verse to downplay receiving the spiritual gifts at all, as if this scripture is saying all you need is love; don't worry about the gifts of the Spirit. Make sure you notice Paul said to "eagerly desire the greater gifts" and he has told us earlier to "pray" specifically for the gift of "prophecy." We are held responsible to use the gifts and talents that God has given us. There are other gifts listed in the Bible and we will look at those too, but for this lesson, I wanted to look at the spiritual gifts and instruction of Paul in I Corinthians. Refer to your worksheet, study it, and respond to it to better understand the gifts of the Spirit, and to begin to recognize where you are gifted.

WEEK SIX WORKSHEETS

Gifts of the Spirit Part I

"He who descended is the one who ascended, that He might fill all things and He gave the apostles, the prophets, the evangelists, the shepherds and teachers, to equip the saints for the work of ministry for building up the body of Christ, till we all come in the unity of the faith, and of the knowledge of the Son of God, unto a perfect man, unto the measure of the stature of the fullness of Christ..." (Ephesians 4:10-13)

Notes:

____

____

____

____

The Purpose of the Spiritual Gifts

To strengthen believers.

To cause unbelievers to believe.

To bring comfort.

To exhort. (To urge earnestly by advice or warning: a sermon)

To edify the church. (give moral or spiritual instruction or improvement.

<u>To place each one of us in our ministry to the rest of the body.</u>

How important is it if you wish to be an effective disciple and do what God is calling you to do to be filled with the Holy Ghost and to examine your natural talents and pray for spiritual gifts? **VERY!** God wants to use you and me to promote His kingdom. He uses our feet, hands, and mouths to do His work in the earth. He **CANNOT** guide us if we do not allow His Spirit a permanent place inside of us, and He **CANNOT** use us the way

He wishes to if we do not understand our gift/gifts of the Spirit and begin to exercise ourselves in the operation of them.

List here your natural talents (things such as good singing voice, teaching ability, ability to play musical instruments, creative with your mind, with organizing, etc.)

____

____

____

____

____

What are the Gifts?
(From I Corinthians 12, 13, 14)

List the spiritual gifts that you believe you are gifted with and have used to help minister to the body:

____

____

____

____

____

Examine again the gifts spoken of in this lesson. Consider the scripture examples given and other personal examples spoken of in this lesson. Write next to each gift any time you have witnessed this gift in a service, in your own life. If you have operated in this gift before, note here the time and circumstance. This is to help you establish where you are particularly gifted. It is also good to recognize that we serve a God who is supernatural, and while the world may not get this, we need to recognize how real the things of the spirit are, and be desiring spiritual gifts from God. We need a powerful and strong church, and this is how we get there. If you have been brought up under a ministry that does not teach being filled with the Holy Ghost, or does not teach these spiritual gifts, you may wish to write questions you wish to have answered beside each of these. You may need to seek out a Spirit-filled pastor to answer your questions, if this lesson has not done so adequately.

1. **The gift of wisdom**: Reference James 1:5-8 and Matthew 16:16-18 (This was Peter's insight from the Father to proclaim Jesus the Christ)

Notes:

____

____

____

____

2. **The gift of knowledge**: Reference John 4:17-18 (Jesus demonstrates a gift of knowledge when He is visiting with the woman who claims she has no husband. Jesus speaks what she is leaving out: that she has had five husbands and is presently living with a man.)

Notes:

____

____

____

____

3. **The gift of faith.** This is a supernatural faith, such as David taking on Goliath with a sling and some rocks. This is the great belief in God. Increase your faith: Read Romans 10:17 and James 1:3.

Notes:

____

____

____

____

4. **The gift of healing**: Reference James 5:14-15 "Is any one of you sick? He should call the elders of the church to pray over him and anoint him with oil in the name of the Lord. And the prayer offered in faith will make the sick person well; the Lord will raise him up. If he has sinned, he will be forgiven."

Notes:

____

____

____

____

5. The gift of miracles: Reference Matthew through John as they give account after account of the miracles wrought by the Lord, and then remember that Jesus said: "Verily, verily, I say unto you, He that believeth on me, the works that I do shall he do also; and greater works than these shall he do; because I go unto my Father." (John 14:12)

Notes:

____

____

____

____

6. The gift of prophecy. Reference I Corinthians Chapter 14. Paul tells us that we should all pray to prophesy. Why? Because this gift matures the church and brings unity to the believers. This is preaching by divine guidance and it is also giving a prophetical utterance.

Notes:

____

____

____

____

7. The gift of distinguishing of spirits. We should all pray and ask the Lord to help us discern spirits in the last days because there will be false prophets and people with wrong spirits we will need to pray for. Understand that the Lord gives this gift to ministers in particular so they can judge situations and be used to help individuals, not to hurt them.

Notes:

____

____

____

____

8. **The gift of tongues.** Initial utterance happens as God fills us with the Holy Ghost. Those who may receive the gift of tongues will speak in languages they do not know fluently, something that is only edifying to them if not done with interpretation. Paul tells us to pray to ourselves and to God if there is not interpretation, and for not more than three message tongues to go forth in a service.

Notes:

____

____

____

____

9. **Interpretation of tongues.** This is the ability to hear a message in a language you have never learned and interpret it for others to understand.

Notes:

____

____

____

____

We are obviously not all called to be apostles, prophets, evangelists, but we are all called to be used in the gift/gifts that God gives to us and to operate in love at all times. God gave us the gifts to build up the church and to perfect the saints. We are all building together when we identify our gifts and allow ourselves to be humbly used of God for His glory and the edifying of His church.

Look through the following list and **identify with an X which ones are talents and with a Y which ones are spiritual gifts; some may be both.** The point is that some natural gene-given talents can be given to the Lord and He can add His Spirit, and those gifts then become supernatural. I have heard people play the piano beautifully, but when someone plays that has had the anointing of God added to his or her talent/s, it brings forth change in people. We want His supernatural gifts, and we want Him to add His Spirit and gift us in any natural talents He has given us.

Playing the piano _______________   Teaching _______________

Preaching _______________   Singing _______________

Assisting the pastor
with any needs _______________   Artistic ability _______________

Oratorical skills _______________   Prophesying _______________

Healings _______________   Wisdom _______________

Knowledge _______________   Athletic ability _______________

Writing ability _______________   Mercy _______________

As you can see, some are natural talents, but can also be spiritual gifts when God adds the gifting of His spirit into it. We want those with "giftings" in these areas to make sure they are using their gift/gifts for the edifying of the church. The Spirit can do so much more than the arm of flesh.

This Week's Challenge

1. Pray and ask the Lord to help you identify your spiritual gift/gifts.

2. Pray and ask the Lord for direction in how He wills for you to help your church and what specific direction He has for your life.

3. Ask someone close to you in church if they recognize any gift in your life that perhaps you are not utilizing.

You probably already know where your gifts lie. Do you want to lose them or use them? We want to USE them!

Memory Verse

"But eagerly desire the greater gifts. And now I will show you the most excellent way." I Corinthians 12:31

WEEK SEVEN

The Gifts of the Spirit Part II

We looked briefly at the five-fold ministry gifts in the previous lesson which included our apostles, prophets, evangelists, pastors and teachers. Our main focus was on the gifts of wisdom, knowledge, faith, healing, tongues, interpretation of tongues, discernment, miracles, and prophecy. We learned that we are to covet spiritual gifts and particularly ask the Lord to give us the gift of prophecy. Whatever spiritual gift or gifts the Lord chooses to bestow on us and use us in, however, we are to be content with those and not wishing we could do what another member is doing. We need to be the member of the body we are called to be, and we need to be operating fully in the gift the Lord has given us. This past week we were supposed to pray for gifts and seek the Lord about how He wishes us to be used in our churches. I hope you did that and that you will continue to do that. Our main objective in the church is to reconcile people to God and to operate in love to one another. We can best do that by allowing the Holy Ghost to operate through us in love _and_ in the spiritual gifts. We are talking this week about some of the service gifts. These are the gifts that members receive in different diversities that help the pastor be able to do his job most effectively, which is praying and preparing sermons and ministering through those sermons. Without the gifts of helps being manifest through different members, he would get bogged down trying to do everything just to keep the church running. So, these gifts are very important: the gifts of leadership, of giving, of helps, of mercy. Before we continue, pray this aloud:

Father, Help me to obey and do all I see in your Word. Help me to acknowledge what your Word is saying to me, even when it runs counter to all I have previously believed and developed as religious tradition. Your Word is full of promises and power, and I wish to obtain and receive all you intend for me to have to be a bold witness and an overcoming Christian. Help me to identify and increase through use all gifts you wish me to use. Forgive me for times I have let others do jobs in your church that you were calling me to do. I know that as I exercise and develop my gifts you will open the doors for their use. I commit myself to you as daughter and servant. Use me, Jesus, for your kingdom's glory. Amen

"We have different gifts, according to the grace given us. If a man's gift is prophesying, let him use it in proportion to his faith. If it is serving, let him serve; if it is teaching, let him teach; if it is encouraging, let him encourage; if it is contributing to the needs of others, let him give generously; if it is leadership, let him govern diligently; if it is showing mercy, let him do it cheerfully." (Romans 1:6-8)

Every Christian should be conducting themselves before others in an upright manner to keep a more powerful witness when sharing their Christian faith with others, and every Christian should be able to teach the plan of salvation to another; we all should be encouraging to each other and giving of our goods to those in need; we all should be good stewards of what goods the Lord has blessed us with, and we should all be able to show mercy and compassion. So, on a natural level, we all are expected to do these gifts as the duties of a Christian, giving and being compassionate. However, we are all aware that some people are gifted in some of these specific areas. Some people are called to work behind the scenes to enable the gospel to be proclaimed. Some of the behind the scenes servants are the ones who are drawing people in to the Lord because of the love that is shown through these gifts. No one may notice you much if you are called in these gifts, but the Lord sees and I do believe the following scripture shows how much God sees things very differently than we see things in the natural.

"But the Lord said to Samuel "Do not consider his appearance or his height, for I have rejected him. The Lord does not look at the things man looks at. Man looks at the outward appearance, but the Lord looks at the heart."
I Samuel 16:7

> "God is looking for servant hearts."

God is looking for servant hearts. God is weighing our heart, looking for a heart that is willing to serve Him and others. In this scripture, the Lord is finished with Saul as king, although he doesn't know it for a while. He is sending Samuel to anoint a new king from Jesse's sons. The first time the principle of the "least being chosen rather than the greatest" is initiated in this scripture. David, the youngest son, still out shepherding, (while his brothers are older, stronger, and already warriors), is the one the Lord chooses. When David is anointed, he is well aware that he has been chosen to be the next king of Israel, but before this actually happens, he is called to serve Saul, and he serves him diligently. There may be times when you know God is calling you to a position, but that doesn't mean tomorrow, so do as David does here. He goes to the kingdom and learns how to be a king **FIRST.** Every trial, betrayal, and attack is working to take David where he has never gone before. God does not pull us out of the filthy world one day and establish us to head up His kingdom the next, or even place us too quickly in any work for Him where we might get lifted up and fail Him through becoming proud. So, whatever God has called you to, understand that trials and tests are part of the program of preparing you to be effective in the work until God says it is **TIME.** Even when Saul turns on David, we see that David never lays a hand on him, even though he has opportunity to kill him. David is a great example of keeping a servant's heart even when he knows he is going to be given an ultimate status as king. No matter what capacity or gift the Lord places in our hearts, we are ultimately servants of the most high God, and servants of one another. No job is too menial to do as unto the Lord. David did not lift himself up, and we should never do that either. We need to practice a servant's heart, and even if we are called to evangelize the world, we should be ready to do whatever needs to be done for the church and each other as we have the capacity to do. With that being said, let's look at the gifting in some of these areas. Everything that is done is done best when God has gifted us to do that area. The gifts are given to us by grace and not according to our own desire or effort, but as God chooses for His purpose and the edifying of His church.

I want to break down each area of service that is talked about in Peter. The first is prophecy. We did talk about this in the previous lesson somewhat, to the extent that we established prophecy is a very important gift because it edifies the church, and that we are all instructed to pray for the gift of prophecy. I Corinthians 12:28 that we referred to in the previous lesson instructs a prophet to use his gift "in proportion to his faith." He needs to be certain he is speaking the words of God and not getting caught up in his enthusiasm and speaking his own thoughts. There are false prophets today who are throwing around a lot of "Thus saith the Lords" who will answer to God for their false prophecies one day. In **Deuteronomy 18:20** there was a punishment for false prophecy: **"But a prophet who presumes to speak in my name anything I have not commanded him to say, or a prophet who speaks in the name of other gods, must be put to death."** The Bible says that the prophets are subject to the prophets, so we know that if we hear anyone proclaiming to be a prophet who is speaking something contrary to the Word of God, he is false. The Word warns us that in the last day many will go to preachers who tickle their ears, rather than receiving sound doctrine. I am trying to give you sound doctrine here. There is a cost to being a Christian. You cannot practice sin. You can be forgiven if you do fall again, but we are supposed to be practicing overcoming. We are learning to be faithful servants because the Word says that the faithful servant will enter heaven and the unprofitable servant will be cast into a lake of fire. (As much as many in the world may wish to believe this is metaphorical, I know the Bible teaches hell, as well as heaven, as a real place, and we get to choose where we will go.)

Serving is mentioned second. Whether you are a pastor serving the people or someone who scrubs the church toilets, serving with all of your heart is very important. The people who are gifted in the area of helps are truly the ones holding up the arms of the pastor at times, because every time they take care of things around the church, or for the people in the church, they free up time to the pastor to pray and prepare for services. We are all working together. The gift of helps may embrace some of the menial jobs and be low-profile at times, but it is not less valuable. God sees everything that is done to further his kingdom, every act of service, and it is the humble heart of service that we see He appreciates in His Word. This type of service is so backward to our world today, but it is so important in the Kingdom of God. If you are gifted with serving, do it joyfully with no expectation of thanks or reward.

Third is teaching. If a person is gifted in the area of teaching, he/she is able to interpret and explain the Bible. Teachers are guided by the hand of the Holy Ghost and instructed by Him as they prepare to teach. They are not going to present teaching the way a preacher preaches. If they are operating in this gift, they, too, are anointed by the power of the Holy Ghost. They may very often operate in the gift of prophecy. Scripture says every disciple should be "apt to teach," so I know the Lord expects all of us to be able to share the plan of salvation with someone else. There may be someone you are able to talk to sometime who never plans to darken the door of a church. You should be able to expound the gospel fully to that person, should a door open for you to do so, to give him/her a true saving knowledge of Jesus Christ. Someone with the gift of teaching will be able to expound, will have a strong desire to study the Word, and prepare and give out teaching.

The fourth thing mentioned in Peter is the gift of encouragement. I have personally had people tell me after purposing to give them specific encouragement that "no one has ever done that sort of thing for me before." The world is hungry for encouragement and it is something that we can all become conscious of and make an effort to do more of simply by thinking about others and how we can encourage them. If you are gifted in this area, it is natural to encourage other Christians, to give a word to the discouraged, to encourage the sinner to repent and turn to Jesus. We will go into more detail of this gift on your worksheet.

There is a gift of giving. This is a spiritual gift not limited to financial giving. There are some, however, who can make money and it is good for them to distribute it to those in need in the church. I have known a poor woman with the gift of giving before. She gave out of her need continually as the woman Jesus observed in scriptures who dropped in the treasury all of her substance. The woman I am referring to was always making dolls for children, giving a substantial amount (for her) to those young people starting out in life in their marriage or following the birth of a child. She simply had a heart for giving. If you have this gift, you are just finding ways to serve every day, giving money, services, talent, and time, whatever you can do to love someone through giving. Giving is not limited to the duty of "tithing." We have really not begun to give until we go beyond tithing because that is duty. Gifted or not, each Christian needs to learn to be a giver and put it into practice. This is a real action that shows you love.

The gift of leadership is very important. Leaders are commanded to "govern diligently." You can't be a leader and take this gift lightly. It is too important to the church and its administration and activities that those chosen to lead know what they are doing and are diligent to follow through. Sometimes the young in church want roles of leadership, but then they don't follow through and show up. That is why you will see ministers being seasoned that take on the pastoring of a church. They have had mentors, they have learned, they understand the seriousness of the leadership of a church. Any of us called to any area of leadership must understand the seriousness of the role, whether it be teaching a Sunday school class, heading up a fellowship dinner, or beginning a bus ministry or youth ministry; the follow up is important, the diligence to the time for preparation and seeking the Lord and His guidance is vital.

The seventh is mercy. The gift of mercy is a gift of compassion. All of us are instructed to be merciful for God has shown us great mercy in delivering us out of sin. Someone with the gift of mercy can just show their compassion in a natural way and with cheerfulness. We are true ambassadors of Christ when we are showing mercy. If you have the gift of mercy, you are able to empathize with people, show kindness, and be compassionate in a great way. You are showing these kindnesses not because you have to but truly from a sincere heart.

In this week's worksheets, I focus on the gifts of mercy and helping. There are some questions there to help us identify these gifts in ourselves. People with the gift of helps may be deacons, cleaners of the church, posters of flyers, door knockers, ushers. If your heart reaches out to the poor, the handicapped, the needy, the elderly, and you feel to help them, you have the gift of mercy. Others of us help out of duty, while you sincerely wish to help alleviate some of the suffering. We all need to pray for more compassion, if we want to be more like Jesus. He lived there! Showing our compassion towards others needs still moves Jesus today, as He was moved when He walked on the earth. Jesus showed mercy again and again; he lived compassion. We need to live compassion.

When we are living in the Spirit, we are doing for others and ignoring our fleshly desires and sometimes our needs. Have you reached the point in your walk with God where you will do without wants to give offerings to your church, to missions, to the neighbor down the street who is out of work, or just lost a precious loved one? Have you reached the point where you give to the man on the street with the cardboard sign asking for help, simply because he is asking for help, rather than saying to yourself, "Why don't you get a job?" I am always reminded of the country song about the man that lost his mind after losing a loved one. I think it is called "Don't Laugh at Me." The few times I have heard it through the years, I can't help but cry and pray that everyone will see others in their hopeless conditions through merciful and compassionate eyes. We don't know why people are where they are or what they have gone through. Don't judge. Just love and be compassionate. Jesus came for the hopeless and the outcast.

When we do these things we are illustrating the gift of mercy. Not only are we meeting others needs, and seemingly, feeling compelled to meet those needs, but we are doing so at cost and risk to our own needs. That is sacrifice--that is compassion--that is mercy. God wants us to keep a balance in our lives, however, so even as we operate in the gifts He has given us, we do not become depleted, and have no more to give. Recognize the need for balance in your lives as you serve, but do serve with all of your heart.

Woman of Faith
Dorcas

"At Joppa there was a certain disciple named Tabitha, which is translated Dorcas. This woman was full of good works and charitable deeds which she did. But it happened in those days that she became sick and died. When they had washed her, they laid her in an upper room. And since Lydda was near Joppa, and the disciples had heard that Peter was there, they sent two men to him, imploring him not to delay in coming to them. Then Peter arose and went with them. When he had come, they brought him to the upper room. And all the widows stood by him weeping, showing the tunics and garments which Dorcas had made while she was with them. But Peter put them all out, and knelt down and prayed. And turning to the body he said,

> "Tabitha, arise." And she opened her eyes, and when she saw Peter she sat up. Then he gave her his hand and lifted her up; and when he had called the saints and widows, he presented her alive. And it became known throughout all Joppa, and many believed on the Lord. (Acts 9: 36-42)

Dorcas was a disciple full of good works and charitable deeds. She was blessed with the gift of helps and mercy. She was full of compassion. We all know that we are not going to be saved by works, but by grace. However, a Christian is known by their fruit of love, and I have found that love worded to others is one thing, but love given and shown through actions gets noticed. We are serving God as Tabita/Dorcas was serving God. At that time, she was evidently an able seamstress, and she gave that talent to the Lord and sewed for the poor. She has probably been giving out of her own need to bless the widows, because it is the widows who are weeping and showing Peter the material blessings of tunics that Dorcas has made for them. We need to be full of good works so that others can see Jesus in us. The world is all about themselves today, what they can get for themselves. You make yourself pretty unusual when you are providing and caring outside the walls of you, yourself, and your own family. This is a witness of love and it helps to draw others to Christ. People feel very alone in this world. Families are alienated by distance, jobs, divorce, drugs, and alcohol abuse. We are the only lifeline some of the people in our communities have. Is it time consuming and exhausting sometimes to show we care? Yes. Is it needful for the harvest of the Lord? Yes.

Colossians 3:17 says, "Whatever you do in word or deed, do all in the name of the Lord Jesus, giving thanks to God the Father through Him."

I want to end this lesson with **Luke 10: 1-8:**

> "After this the Lord appointed seventy-two others and sent them two by two ahead of Him to every town and place where he was about to go. He told them, "The harvest is plentiful, but the workers are few. Ask the Lord of the harvest, therefore, to send out workers into his harvest field. <u>Go!</u> I am sending you out like lambs among wolves. Do not take a purse, or bag or sandals; and do not greet anyone on the road. When you enter a house, first say "Peace to this house. If a man of peace is there, your

> peace will rest on him; if not, it will return to you. Stay in
> that house, eating and drinking whatever they give you,
> for the worker deserves his wages. Do not move around
> from house to house. When you enter a town and are
> welcomed, eat what is set before you."

These workers are being sent out before Jesus to prepare the way for the gospel. You and I are out in his fields today making relationship with people out in the world to prepare a way for Jesus to enter their heart; we extend our friendship, our help, our comfort to them, and they begin to see that we are different, and that difference is the love of God flowing through us to them. The workers in the above scriptures are sent out by twos, and I believe there is so much more power than we realize when we pray by twos and work by twos. I know that there is a need today to utilize the most effective ways to get the world evangelized. Several keys to effective harvest of souls are in these scriptures.

1. That we purpose to become workers in the harvest and GO!

2. That we work in multiples of two for greatest benefit, and

3. That we are careful to be content and not offend as we are working.

I know missionaries who have eaten horrendous things so as not to offend the people offering the food. Not receiving hospitality can be offensive. Be gracious to receive people's gifts no matter how humble. Americans are so spoiled. I have asked people to dinner at my house, and they have asked what I would be having before they would accept the invitation. I have had young people at my house who have declined my full course meal and ran to McDonald's for chicken nuggets and brought them back and ate them at the table as we were clearing the dishes. I just shook my head and laughed, but perhaps we should recognize the need to teach our children how to be gracious and thankful. Other people would have gotten offended.

Find a prayer and a work partner for the things of the Lord, someone who can encourage you and will be equally committed to continue in good works for the Lord. I don't know that I have ever officially told one of the elder saints in my church that she is my prayer partner; we simply call each other and share our needs and pray together, and report to one another that God is moving in those situations. I feel more strength when someone else is helping me pray. I sometimes feel the prayers of my church when

I have a need and they sincerely pray believing for the need. I believe in the power of two or more praying and asking of the Lord. We still need our prayer closets, and we should be praying for our needs and the needs of others, and not calling the pastor each day and troubling him to pray for us. He is already compelled to pray for the entire church. The power of two--Jesus told us "where two or more agree, as touching anything, it would be done"--study together, pray together, give Bible studies together, and witness together. It will become more powerful the deeper you go with it. If we want to help in the harvest, we need to learn to be effective as laborers. We need to capitalize on each other's gifts, and we need to be strong and unified in every act of evangelism.

I wanted to make us aware of the gifts of the Spirit, not only for the purpose of seeking and utilizing those gifts, but so we are aware that God needs us to be full of His Holy Spirit, needs us to be led by His Spirit, and needs us to begin to act to recognize, use, and exercise those gifts. Remember that talents are natural and need to be given to the Lord for His use, but gifts are spiritual and are placed in us by God at the time of our spiritual birth. They are placed there to be used. They are placed there to minister to others in your church. They are placed there to move the unbeliever into believing. Our flesh cannot do this: His Spirit can. We are His body; He can't do it without us. He needs us, just as we need Him.

Week Seven Worksheets

The Gifts of the Spirit Part II

"We have different gifts, according to the grace given us. If a man's gift is prophesying, let him use it in proportion to his faith. If it is serving, let him serve; if it is teaching, let him teach; if it is encouraging, let him encourage; if it is contributing to the needs of others, let him give generously; if it is leadership, let him govern diligently; if it is showing mercy, let him do it cheerfully." (Romans 12:6-8)

Recall: We are instructed to "covet" spiritual gifts, but to particularly ask to ____.

Why?

____

____

Even if you do not particularly feel called in the gift of helps or mercy, what do you see in the above scriptures that we all should be doing as Christians. List those things here.

____

____

____

"But the Lord said to Samuel 'Do not consider his appearance or his height, for I have rejected him. The Lord does not look at the things man looks at. Man looks at the outward appearance, but the Lord looks at the heart.'" (I Samuel 16:7)

Don't be modest and don't be proud, but write here what you believe the Lord can see in your heart. Be honest. Write the good. Write the bad. It's not like the Lord can't see.

____

____

____

David represents in the Old Testament what Jesus made all of us who believe in Him in this dispensation--a king and a servant. We have been made both kings and priests by Jesus Christ, and Jesus ultimately represented being both master and servant while on this earth. We have to get the servanthood right to be effective in His kingdom. One of his kingdom principles is "the least among you shall be the greatest." David was the least of his brothers, but he became the great King David. So, don't be afraid of serving here and not being recognized. God sees it all. Do an accountability check here.

How am I serving God?

____

____

What talents have I been given naturally am I submitting to God's service?

____

____

____

In what ways? Be specific.

____

____

Do I recognize spiritual gifts that the Lord is using me in? List them.

____

____

Let's Examine This Week's Study of Gifts

<u>Prophecy</u>--From I Corinthians 12:28, studied last week, we learned the prophet must use his gift "in proportion to his faith." He needs to be certain he is speaking the words of God and not getting caught up in his own enthusiasm. A warning was issued to false prophets in the Old Testament. "But a prophet who presumes to speak in my name anything I have not commanded him to say, or a prophet who speaks in the name of other gods, must be put to death." Deuteronomy 18:20. It is a serious thing to say "Thus saith the Lord" when He didn't. You can recognize false prophets today because the "prophets are subject

to the prophet." If a prophet comes to us speaking things that do not line up with the Word of God, he/she is a false prophet. The Apostle Paul instructed to "let them be accursed" that would come preaching any other doctrine than what he had already taught.

Do you know of a prophet that has come since the apostles and taught some new thing and caused people to go astray?

____

____

<u>Serving</u>--The idea of serving others is a pretty backward way of thinking in our present world, but in God's Kingdom it is a requirement. The gift of service helps hold up the arms of our pastors, as Moses arms were held up in the O.T. If we want to have victory in our lives, and in our churches, we will all find and use our gifts, and if we are gifted in the area of service, we are blessed. Do not find anything menial that is done to further the work of Jesus. You are blessed and a blessing when you serve others. When natural talents are turned into spiritual gifts, it frees others to use the public gifts, like preaching, teaching, or being a missionary. It is important. Do you see the service gifts for the valuable help that they are to others? Do you have the gift of helping people?

Answer the following:

1. Do you know that God has placed you in your church specifically to help free up time for your minister to do his job?

____

____

2. Are you okay doing the routine jobs that need to be done at church that some would find tedious?

____

____

3. Do you like being behind the scenes rather than out in front?

____

____

4. Do you actually like doing cooking, sewing, office work, decorating, maintenance, or ushering?

____

____

If so, do the work of serving with a joyful attitude. It is your gift and a much needed and appreciated one to your pastor.

We discussed the gift of teaching in last week's lesson as well. Someone with the gift of teaching will be able to explain the Word, will have a strong desire to study the Word, and prepare and give out the Word. We should all be able to teach the gospel message of salvation to someone. You should take time to think that through.

Can you teach the salvation message to someone else? <u>Write down what you would say and the scriptures you would direct them to.</u> If you do nothing else on this worksheet, do this, because this is what we are ultimately called to do, each of us, as disciples of the Lord Jesus Christ. We are called to share the gospel and tell people how to be saved. We need to make sure we aren't giving them only half of the message.

____

____

____

<u>Fourth, is the gift of encouragement.</u> We all should consciously practice this, but some are gifted in this especially. Encouragement is priceless. It keeps us from giving up. Here is a list of ways to encourage people. Tell them they are doing a good job; tell them the Lord will help them in their need; write a note to encourage someone who is down, who needs sympathy. Notice those in church who look down and make sure you take time to speak to them, give them a hug, and follow up during the week with a phone call. Give your time to them. That is very meaningful in a very busy world. Make your own list below of those you want to take time to encourage and write specifically how you intend to do so. You may be the source of inspiration to someone who has never had a source. Do it as unto the Lord.

Person　　　　　　**What I will do for them this week**

____

____

Fifth, the gift of giving. It's not just about the money. Do examine the following as a spiritual check in this area, however. Am I tithing 10% to my church? If not, how can I get there?

Do I also give offering to my church?

Do I give of my finances to others less fortunate than myself?

How much time do I give the Lord in prayer?

How much time do I give to the study of His Word?

How much time do I spend doing things for my family, my church, for others? (Break it down, truly calculate it)

Am I keeping my life balanced as I help? My family relationships are guarded, rather than sacrificed?

Leadership as a gift of the spirit is so needful and the commitment to service that must go with it. Are you a leader? In what areas? Examine any areas of service that you have a passion about, and you will probably find the area where you have leadership ability. (if this is your gift and calling).

____

____

____

The seventh gift tonight that we are studying is mercy. A gift of compassion. You may have the gift of mercy if you respond with a yes to any of the following questions. While the gift of helps releases those with speaking gifts to do their job more effectively, the gift of mercy is directed more to the needy in our society: the outcasts.

1. Do you have compassion for people bound by drugs?

____

____

2. Do you feel love and a desire to give to the poor, the depressed, those in prison, those who cannot give you anything back for your efforts?

____

____

3. Are you known for responding to others' needs?

____

____

If you have a compassion for others that prompts you to aid them, not just occasionally, but all of the time, you have a gift of mercy. The Lord bless you. We all need to practice compassion and reaching out to those in need.

Read Acts 9: 36-42

Are you a Dorcas? Explain. If not, what Bible woman would you pattern yourself after or have the most desire to emulate?

____

____

This Week's Challenges

I challenge all of us to pray and ask God to direct us to be doing in His service those things that He has made us and purposed for us to do. Lay aside our wants and desires for recognition and just serve Him in whatever capacity He leads us to.

I challenge us to do good works for others this week, not just to be doing, but to be serving Jesus as Women of F.A.I.T.H.

I challenge us to pray for others and for revival and deliverance in our communities and nation.

Do these three specific things this week:

1. Call your pastor's wife and ask her if there is anything you need to do for her or the church. Tell her you appreciate and love her.

2. If you have never practiced praying with your family except at dinner, ask them to spend some time together in the evening for a devotional time with the Word and prayer. Ask them if they have needs they want the family to pray about. If you are a single woman, find another lady in church that you can touch base with for a few moment's each day and share prayer needs, and agree to pray for each other's prayer requests daily.

3. If there is something you have been wanting to do at church, tell your pastor and ask him to pray about it (if you are truly feeling led by the Lord to do this--do not get hurt feelings if he doesn't respond for a while--you may not be the right person at this time. Still, he will know you are interested if it comes around again).

Memory Verse

"This woman was full of good works and
charitable deeds which she did." Acts 9:37

WEEK EIGHT

Women's Roles in the Church

We have some scriptures in the Bible that cause controversy many times concerning the role of women in the church today. I have sought the Lord for an explanation many times concerning some of these scriptures because I believe the understanding of these scriptures must be misunderstood or taken out of context for the disunity to exist about what women can or cannot do in the church. We came across one of these scriptures in our study week before last in I Corinthians where if we take the verses literally without looking into the complete context of what was happening in the church these were being written to, then women are not supposed to sing in church, say "Amen, "teach Sunday school, teach in the assembly or preach, pray, or prophesy, instruct their children to be quiet, etc. If this is what Paul is actually saying, then he is contradicting what he has said in Corinthians 11, where he instructs the women, as well as the men, how to pray and prophesy in the church. He is not contradicting himself. We need to understand that he is speaking to a church out of order in I Corinthians 14, and bringing order to that church by requiring that the women submit to the men's leadership. There aren't contradictions in the Bible; but when there seems to be, we must compare scriptures, compare what was happening in the Old Testament, in that day's culture, and what they are specifically addressing, if it is for us or for that time. The Lord changed some things after Calvary. Some of those things went against what the cultures were used to. We have to look at the context of what was happening in each of the churches that Paul is addressing. I want to look at the difficult scriptures first, then go on to put them in cultural context, so they do not contradict what Paul has said before, what has been prophesied in Joel will come to the church, or what happened at Pentecost when women, as well as men, received the Holy Ghost and spake in tongues. If God did not want women to speak in the church at any point ever, He would have to keep us from being filled with the Holy Ghost, never use a woman to speak in tongues or interpret; in effect, many of the spiritual gifts would be for men alone, which would contradict other scriptures. We want to be used fully by the Lord, but we can't be used fully if we misunderstand what is happening and what is really being said in these scriptures. We don't change scriptures, add to scriptures, or throw out scriptures, but we do rightly divide the Word of God and let the instruction work together. Let's look at the scriptures.

"Let your women keep silent in the churches, for they are not permitted to speak; but they are to be submissive, as the law also says. And if they want to learn something let them ask their own husbands at home; for it is shameful for women to speak in church." (I Corinthians 14:34-36)

We read I Corinthians chapters 12, 13, and 14 in our study of gifts of the Spirit Week Six, so you remember that Paul is addressing a church that every time they come together they all have a psalm, a tongue, an interpretation, a teaching, women as well as men. So, to get order in that church, at a time when women were not educated, but God has poured His Spirit out on them also, Paul backs up to headship order, which has not passed away with the law. The wives are still subject to their husbands, and Paul uses that to bring order to the confusion in this church. This is a beginning church with lots of questions and they can't email Paul and get a response in five minutes. They are writing their questions and sending them to Paul and Paul is reading the questions and probably reading between the lines before he answers and sends his replies. The women in this church were possibly being very disruptive because they wanted to understand and learn, and that is now open to them through the work of the Holy Ghost, but still not in a disorderly way in the church. If everyone that came into a church wanted to share what God had revealed to them that week or was trying to use their gift to edify the church instead of waiting on the others it had been revealed to, they could never get to the preaching. Paul has to instruct them to control the gifts somewhat for there to be order. He is not saying the women cannot be used by God, but that they need to let the men be first, be submissive, and be quiet in the church, rather than noisy, asking questions and interrupting during church. These were uneducated women with a lot of questions and they were evidently interrupting the men who were not their husbands to ask questions about the Lord and the church. They may have even been challenging the male teachers. It was chaos, so Paul told them to keep quiet and to save their questions for their husbands at home to bring order to the church. Paul concludes with **verse 39**, saying, **"Therefore, brethren, desire earnestly to prophesy, and do not forbid to speak with tongues. Let all things be done decently and in order."** He is instructing the women to allow the men to have leadership, and to keep the service orderly, waiting to ask questions of their husbands at home. They are still under male leadership, but if the Lord moved on a woman to give a tongues and interpretation, as well as a man, he is instructing them not to forbid tongues.

> "But I want you to know that the head of every man is Christ, the head of woman is man, and the head of Christ is God. Every man praying or prophesying, having his head covered, dishonors his head. But every woman who prays or prophesies with her head uncovered dishonors her head, for that is one and the same as if her head were shaved. For if a woman is not covered, let her also be shorn. But if it is shameful for a woman to be shorn or shaved, let her be covered. For a man indeed ought not to cover his head, since he is the image and glory of God; but woman is the glory of man. For man is not from woman, but woman from man. Nor was man created for the woman, but woman for the man. For this reason the woman ought to have a symbol of authority on her head, because of the angels. Nevertheless, neither is man independent of woman, nor woman independent of man, in the Lord. For as woman came from man, even so man also comes through woman; but all things are from God."
> (I Corinthians 11:3-16)

This praying or prophesying that Paul is instructing how it should be done is also to women, who would have to speak aloud in church to prophesy, so the subsequent instruction to the church at Corinth for women to be silent in the church in Chapter 14 has to be a chastisement for a church that has already been identified as unruly earlier in the chapter. God may use men or women to prophesy, but there is still an order: God over man, and man over woman, so the woman should show she is submissive to that order of authority. It does not mean that she cannot prophesy in the church if the Lord wills to use her to do so.

Another verse that seems to say that women cannot speak in the church is found in **I Timothy 1:8-15:**

> "I desire therefore that the men pray everywhere, lifting up holy hands, without wrath and doubting; in like manner also, that the women adorn themselves in modest apparel, with propriety and moderation, not with braided hair or gold or pearls or costly clothing, but, which is proper for women professing godliness, with good works. Let a woman learn in silence with all submission. And I do not permit a woman to teach or to have authority over a man, but to be in silence. For Adam was formed first, then Eve. And Adam was not deceived, but the woman being deceived, fell into transgression. Nevertheless she will be saved in childbearing if they continue in faith, love, and holiness, with self-control."

These scriptures are about how women should learn and respect their male authority, not about preventing them from ever teaching. They are to be silent while **learning**, and not challenge the authority of a male authoritative teacher in public. Even the women we will look at in the New Testament who had a teaching role did so under the authority of a man! Priscilla was under the authority of her husband Aquila. There were women who shared in Paul's ministry who were under his authority, and the daughters of Phillip who were said to prophesy were under their father. We have all known women who can't be told anything; they want to argue to have the last say about things. When Paul is instructing Timothy about the order of things, he is instructing a young minister about conduct for the church and keeping the order of authority right. The women need to learn in silence (not interrupting or questioning or challenging the male authority in the church). He goes on to instruct women not to try to teach or have authority over a man, but to be in silence. A woman is out of order is she tries to **dominate** the men and take authority over them to teach them. We need to see if keeping that order of authority prevents all teaching according to the Word of God, according to **ALL** of the scripture's examples.

Joel 2:28 says, "And it shall come to pass afterward that I will pour out My spirit on all flesh; Your sons and your daughters shall prophesy, Your old men shall dream dreams, Your young men shall see visions. And also on My menservants and on My maidservants I will pour out My Spirit in those days." We are living in the days when God is pouring out His Spirit, and this scripture says on **all flesh, sons and daughters shall prophesy.**

Prophesy is speaking the things of God before others. When God's Spirit is poured out on men and women, they are both speaking aloud in church in tongues, interpretation of tongues, and prophesy. Again, Paul has to be saying in I Corinthians to have orderliness and quietness, rather than to be commanding the women never to speak in tongues or to prophesy, although in that particular church where there was unruliness, he was telling the women in particular to let the men speak first and control themselves.

Look at **Acts 2:1-4: "And when the day of Pentecost was fully come, they were all with one accord in one place. And suddenly there came a sound from heaven as of a rushing mighty wind, and it filled all the house where they were sitting. And there appeared to them cloven tongues like as of fire, and it sat upon each of them. And they were all filled with the Holy Ghost, and began to speak with other tongues, as the Spirit gave them utterance."** Those in the upper room we learned earlier in scripture included 120 men and women, the disciples, Mary, other women, and Jesus' brothers. They all spoke with tongues. God did not just send His Spirit to men, but He poured His Spirit out on women too, just as Joel the prophet had prophesied. Women being baptized with the Holy Ghost in this dispensation changed the role of women. Before Jesus ascended and sent the Holy Ghost to us, we see Him beginning to give an example of different treatment of women and Gentiles. He allows a prostitute to wash His feet; He allows Mary of Bethany to sit and learn at His feet; He sends Mary to instruct the male disciples that He has risen: He teaches the woman at the well about the "waters of life He alone can provide." He does not reveal just how wide He is opening the door for women until after He dies, rises, ascends to heaven, and sends the Holy Ghost to women, as well as men. Women are his disciples too and anything His Spirit instructs us to do should line up with the Word of God; we should understand and rightly divide the Word of God. We were all made kings and priests and can all be used as the Lord wills. If we want to be used, however, we need to understand He did not lift the order of submission to Him and to the men as leaders of the church. That does not mean that the women cannot have a leadership role; it simply means that they are still under the headship of men, as well as God. For a woman to teach the Word of God, to be allowed to teach the Word of God, she should follow the guidance of the Holy Ghost, and keep herself in submission to the authority over her. Many of our churches are still uncomfortable with a woman preaching and teaching in the assembly, but if the Lord calls a woman to do this, she, as well as others, should recognize that call.

"For you are all sons of God through faith in Christ Jesus. For as many of you as were baptized into Christ have put on Christ. There is neither Jew nor Greek, there is neither slave nor free, there is neither male nor female; for you are all one in Christ Jesus." (Galatians 3:26-28) We see an equalization happening in this dispensation from these verses that came about from being baptized into Christ. The baptism of the Holy Ghost equalized things for men and women, yet from other scriptures we see that God still means for men to maintain a headship over the women as ordered from the beginning.

Titus 2:3-4 says, "the older women likewise, that they be reverent in behavior, not slanderers, not given to much wine, teachers of good things--that they admonish the young women to love their husbands, to love their children…" Women can teach the aspects of Christian women's conduct more appropriately than men. I know that I enjoy all of the preaching I have heard from our male ministers, but there are a few women Bible teachers that I have learned so much from, because simply by being a woman, they understand the problem areas prevalent in our sex, and can teach best how to overcome some of those problem areas better than the men. This is not taking authority over a man. One Bible teacher that I enjoy listening to and have learned a lot from is careful to state that her husband is over her, as well as her pastor.

I also believe that the men who listen to this teaching learn a lot about God, plus get a better handle on understanding their women. The baptism of the Holy Ghost equalized things for men and women, yet from other scriptures we see that God still means for men to maintain a headship over the women as ordered from the beginning. Consider this a moment: when Peter went to teach Cornelius and his family about Jesus, and the Holy Ghost fell on them while they were preaching, Peter did not say, "Well, that is going against scripture. This should just be for the Jews." He observed God was baptizing them with His Spirit, and they had just stepped into the church same as the Holy Ghost filled Jewish believers. He said then that they could not be denied being baptized with water, too, in the name of the Lord. So, when the Holy Ghost was first being given, and the men who were used to dominating in everything at all times beheld the women receiving the Holy Ghost, too, they had to do some reevaluating, too, didn't they? If God fills a man or a woman with His Spirit today, He can operate through either one as **He wills,** can't He?

If the pastor asks you to pray in church or sing, you are not taking authority over the men in the service, but rather are being under authority to the pastor. There are people who have tried to take the verses in I Corinthians 14 and II Timothy and even keep women from singing in church because there is instruction in the songs, in psalms and hymns.

Colossians 3:16 says, "Let the Word of Christ dwell in you richly, in all wisdom; teaching and admonishing one another in spiritual songs singing with grace in your hearts to the Lord."

These instructions are to the church, men and women, and we know that women are often anointed to sing, and we are moved and admonished at times through their singing as well as many males. If the instructions in I Corinthians 14 and II Timothy are meant to actually be telling women never to open their mouth in the assembly at church, as some wish to claim today, (if those instructions were to be followed literally today), all of the women reading this right now who have worked in church in any fashion have broken that instruction. If you have taught Sunday school, taught a Bible study in church such as this, sung in front of church or even congregationally, which is speaking out, or prayed out loud in church in tongues aloud, or testified or prophesied, you would have broken I Corinthians instructions in chapter 14, if what Paul meant was for women to never open their mouth in church. We have to rightly divide the Word of God, and we have to discern the meaning of the whole counsel of God's Word, rather than all women avoiding doing what God may be calling us to do because of misunderstanding the context of scripture and what is actually being said about women being silent in the church in I Corinthians and II Timothy. On a cautionary note, we need to understand that God calls men and women to do work for Him, but if we are trying to call ourselves or raise ourselves to a position He does not desire us to be in, it will fail.

Let us look at some women in the New Testament who had leadership roles while staying under the authority of men. Priscilla helped her husband

Aquila expound the gospel more perfectly to Apollo (she would have been teaching a man) under the authority of her husband. Paul salutes her and her husband several times in his letters. Many women in the New Testament are referred to as fellow soldiers, fellow prisoners, fellowlaborers. The Apostle Paul salutes the women who labored with him in Romans 16:7 (Junia) and Romans 16:3 (Priscilla). Phebe is given the description of a word (diakonon) that means "deacon," or "minister," or "servant."

Anna is mentioned as a prophetess in the New Testament, but it is before the Holy Ghost is given. She is the one prophesying in the temple concerning who Jesus is and the atonement he will bring to this people. In the Old Testament, we have several women mentioned who did prophesy. Deborah was a prophetess and judge in Israel, so she would have had authority to speak God's Word to men and women. Huldah was a prophetess. Elizabeth and other women spoke prophetically in the Bible. They may not all have operated in the position of "prophetess," but they were used to speak profound things, so it cannot be said that it is never recorded in scripture that women are used to speak the things of God, and those of us who have received the Holy Ghost should understand that if we are being led by the Spirit of God, we are the sons of God, or in the feminine, the daughters of God.

If a woman wants to be used of God, will keep her attitude one of submission not only to God, but to the male leadership over her; if she will be faithful, study to show herself approved, and if it be the will of God to use her, God will open a door that no man will close.

Woman of Faith
Deborah

"Now Deborah, a prophetess, the wife of Lapidoth, was judging Israel at that time. And she would sit under the palm tree of Deborah between Ramah and Bethel in the mountains of Ephraim. And the children of Israel came up to her for judgments. Then she sent and called for Barak the son of Abinoam from Kedesh in Naphtali, and said to him, "Has not the Lord God of Israel commanded, "Go and deploy troops at Mount Tabor; take with you ten thousand men of the sons of Naphtali and of the sons of Zebulun;

and against you I will deploy Sisera, the commander of Jabin's army, with his chariots and his multitude at the River Kishon; and I will deliver him into your hand?" And Barak said to her, "If you will go with me, then I will go; but if you will not go with me, I will not go!" So she said, "I will surely go with you; nevertheless there will be no glory for you in the journey you are taking, for the LORD will sell Sisera into the hand of a woman. Then Deborah arose and went with Barak to Kedesh. And Barak called Zebulun and Naphtali to Kedesh; he went up with ten thousand men under this command, and Deborah went up with him." (Judges 4:4-14)

Before the ensuing battle is over, it is as Deborah has prophesied; Sisera is given into the hands of a woman; for it is Jael that takes a hammer and drives a peg into Sisera's temple. You can read the song of Deborah **in Judges 5:1-31.** The second verse says, "**When leaders lead in Israel, When the people willingly offer themselves, Bless the Lord!**" And it is the woman, Jael, who is saluted in this song of victory in battle. So, we see a woman in the Old Testament, who was not only used as a prophetess, but as a judge, who commanded a man and went with him to battle. We also see the Lord using another woman by the name of Jael, and giving her the opportunity for victory over Sisera.

> "When leaders lead in Israel, when the people willingly offer themselves, Bless the Lord!"

I think I would just conclude by saying we see men used in authority in the Old and New Testaments as leaders, but we also see that when God chooses to use a woman, it is not a big deal; it is accepted. It may be the exception that we see in the Bible, but it is happening. If we want God to use us, He will if we are faithful and we empty ourselves out so that He can use us. As it says in the second verse of Deborah's song"**...when the people willingly offer themselves...Bless the Lord!" Great victories can be won when we give ourselves willingly to the Lord to be used.**

WEEK EIGHT WORKSHEETS

Women's Roles in the Church

This study is to rightly divide the Word of God concerning women's roles in the church.

> **"Let your women keep silent in the churches, for they are not permitted to speak; but they are to be submissive, as the law also says. And if they want to learn something, let them ask their own husbands at home; for it is shameful for women to speak in church."**
> **I Corinthians 14:34-36**

What did we learn in the lesson about the cultural context of what was happening in this church in Corinth?

____

____

Have you felt led to do something by God but have held back because of a learned tradition about women's roles in the church, out of fear of those who hold those traditions, or because you have only looked at these scriptures alone, rather than rightly dividing the Word of God, comparing scriptures with scriptures?

____

____

Has this study changed your mind about anything? Or did you already have a correct understanding of the roles of women in the church of God?

____

____

> **"But I want you to know that the head of every man is Christ, the head of woman is man, and head of Christ is God. Every man praying or prophesying, having his head covered, dishonors his head. But every woman who prays or prophesies with her head uncovered dishonors her head, for that is one and the same as if her head were shaved." (I Corinthians 11:3-5)**

Do you understand that the man or the woman praying or prophesying is doing so aloud in church?

____

____

____

Pray about these scriptures and ask the Lord to help you honor His authority and that of your husband's or spiritual leaders at all times. Then you will be ready to be used.

> **"I desire therefore that the men pray everywhere, lifting up holy hands, without wrath and doubting; in like manner also, that the women adorn themselves in modest apparel, with propriety and moderation, not with braided hair or gold or pearls or costly clothing, but, which is proper for women professing godliness, with good works. Let a woman learn in all silence with submission. And I do not permit a woman to teach or to have authority over a man, but to be in silence. For Adam was formed first, then Eve. And Adam was not deceived, but the woman being deceived, fell into transgression. Nevertheless she will be saved in childbearing if they continue in faith, love, and holiness, with self-control." (I Timothy I:8-15)**

I explain the above scripture to be telling women to "LEARN" in silence, and not to try to take authority over a man that is teaching. If you are a woman who has been studying the Word of God for twenty years, sitting under the hearing of anointed men and women of God as they preach and teach, and a young man comes along wanting to know about the Lord, do you believe you are qualified to teach him the things of God, to share the salvation message with him, or do you feel you need to take him and find another man to teach him about the things of God?

____

____

____

____

In the Word of God, both Aquila and his wife, Priscilla, were expounding the Word to Apollos, teaching him the way more "perfectly." He already was teaching what he knew, but he did not have all of the revelation concerning Jesus, and it was Priscilla, as well as her husband, that taught it to him.

Examine what you believe the Lord is calling you to do in the body of Christ. Record that here:

____

____

Are you afraid to do what you feel called to do?

____

____

Why?

____

____

"And it shall come to pass afterward That I will pour out My Spirit on all flesh; Your sons and your daughters shall prophesy, Your old men shall dream dreams, Your young men shall see visions. And also on My menservants and on My maidservants I will pour out My Spirit in those days." (Joel 2:28)

Do you believe the above prophecy is true?

____

____

Do you believe these are the last days?

____

____

Have you received the baptism of the Holy Ghost?

____

____

Have you prophesied?

____

____

Are you open to be filled by God and led by God?

____

____

THEN HE CAN USE YOU! JUST LET HIM USE YOU! SAY IT! USE ME, LORD!

"For you are all sons of God through faith in Christ Jesus. For as many of you as were baptized into Christ have put on Christ; there is neither Jew nor Greek, there is neither slave nor free, there is neither male nor female; for you are all one in Christ Jesus." (Galatians 3:26-28) If men and women who have faith in Christ Jesus are one in Him, then Jesus can surely use any of His body in any way He wishes. Where we had select men and women in the Old Testament who were moved on by the Holy Ghost and spoke as the oracles of God, since Jesus ascended to Heaven and sent the Holy Ghost to reside in those who believe and obey Him, we have now all been made kings and priests. The Lord may stir up His Spirit in many of us to speak for Him as He wills. He has not left the women out of the speaking gifts, but has still ordained the submission order of the women being under the men.

Can God separate himself from His Spirit? If it is His Spirit speaking through us, is that Spirit any less qualified because it speaks through the lips of a woman rather than a man?

____

____

The real question is, are we being led by the Spirit in what we are doing, or are we being led by our flesh?

____

____

Are we calling ourselves to do a work, or is God?

____

____

Do you remember what my F.A.I.T.H. acronym stands for?

____

____

Do you understand what it means?

____

Let God initiate by the Holy Ghost in you the actions He wants you to perform daily, and the service He is calling you to in the body of Christ. If He is going to do it THROUGH you, you will not fail. If it is YOU doing it, YOU CANNOT SUCCEED! Remember, when God opens a door, no man can close it!

F.A.I.T.H.
FAITHFUL ACTIONS INITIATED THROUGH HIM.

We have to rightly divide the Word of God, and we have to discern the meaning of the whole counsel of God's Word, rather than all women avoiding doing what God may be calling us to do because of misunderstanding the context and what is actually being said about women being silent in the church in I Corinthians and II Timothy.

Women Who Had Leadership Roles

Deborah-judge and prophetess
Anna-prophetess
Huldah-Prophetess
Priscilla-Co-teacher with husband
Phebe--May have been a deacon, a minister, or a servant
Elizabeth--wife of prophet; she also spoke
prophetically when she saw Mary
Sarah--wife of Abraham
Mary and other women-spoke with tongues on the day of Pentecost
Martha-spoke prophetically of the Lord
Other women mentioned as fellow prisoners,
fellowlabourers, fellow soldiers, and helpers in the New
Testament were Junia, Apphia, Tryphena, Tryphosa.

If a woman wants to be used of God, will keep her attitude one of submission not only to God, but to the male leadership over her, if she will be faithful, study to show herself approved, and if it be the will of God to use her, God will open a door. In conclusion, God uses men in authority in the Old and New Testaments as leaders, but we also see that when God chooses to use a woman, it is no big deal; it is accepted. In the Old Testament, it was the exception. In the beginning of the New Testament church, there were many cultural restraints and biases, as well as lack of education for women at that time. Today, we have the Word available to men and women; we have the Spirit of God residing in obedient and faithful men and women. The Holy Ghost will lead those who will hear and follow. I think anything is possible with God if women want to be used to glorify the King today.

**When leaders lead…when people willingly
offer themselves…Just serve Him!!**

This Week's Challenge
Read the song of Deborah in Judges 5:1-31.

Give yourself completely to God for any role in the body of Christ He wishes you to fill. Completely! Write Jesus a letter telling Him you are completely His!

If you know the song, "Exclusively Yours," sing it to Him.

Memory Verse

**"There is neither Jew nor Greek, there is neither bond
nor free, there is neither male nor female: for ye are all
one in Christ Jesus." Galatians 3:28**

WEEK NINE

Don't Lose What He Speaks to Your Heart

Woman of Faith
Mary, Mother of Jesus

"But Mary kept all these things, and pondered them in her heart." Luke 2:19

Pray this aloud: Father, I pray that Your Will would be accomplished in earth as in heaven. I am asking for strength and courage today that I will not let you down, but will receive and obey all instructions from Your Word, and will listen and heed all that Your Spirit speaks to me. I pray for your strength that I will run this race set before me to bring You glory and honor. Help me to present myself to you as Mary did--a handmaid in your service and at your service. Be it unto me as You desire to give to me. Help me to trust You with that kind of faith. Increase my faith, Lord. Amen

Mary, the mother of our Lord is whom I want to study about this week as our woman of faith. The verse in **Luke 2:19** has often fascinated me, and I wanted to discuss and bring out everything that this young girl may have faced when the angel appears to her, appears to a simple young girl who is espoused to Joseph, of the house of David. During the sixth month of Elisabeth's pregnancy with John the Baptist, this angel appears to Mary:

> "And the angel came in unto her, and said, Hail, thou
> that art highly favored, the LORD is with thee; blessed

> art thou among women. And when she saw him, she was troubled at his saying, and cast in her mind what manner of salutation this should be. And the angel said unto her, Fear not, Mary: for thou hast found favour with God… and, behold, thou shalt conceive in thy womb, and bring forth a son, and shalt call his name JESUS. He shall be great, and shall be called the Son of the Highest: and the Lord God shall give unto him the throne of his father David: and he shall reign over those of Jacob for ever; and of his kingdom there shall be no end. Then said Mary unto the angel, How shall this be, seeing I know not a man?" (Luke 1:28-34)

Isn't that an interesting response for a young virgin girl? Not, "I don't think so. Mom and Dad aren't going to buy this, and Joseph will never marry me if I suddenly come up pregnant.' No, she asks how it can possibly happen.

> "And the angel answered and said unto her, the Holy Ghost shall come upon thee, and the power of the Highest shall overshadow thee: therefore also that holy thing which shall be born of thee shall be called the Son of God. And behold, thy cousin Elisabeth, she hath also conceived a son in her old age: and this is the sixth month with her, who was called barren. For with God nothing shall be impossible. And Mary said, Behold the handmaid of the Lord; be it unto me according to thy word. And the angel departed from her." (Luke 1: 35-38)

I can imagine the young Mary "pondering" in her heart all of this. *'Let's see, I'm not married to Joseph yet; I'm a virgin; an angel says I am about to become pregnant and birth a child to be named JESUS who will be great, called the Son of the Highest, who will inherit the throne of his father David, and of his kingdom there shall be no end. I will conceive this child by the Holy Ghost. Okay. Be it unto thy handmaid according to thy Word. I am willing to risk all of the persecution this is going to bring forth to be highly favored of God and a part of this great thing that I can't even wrap my mind around. My heart and my faith have gotten hold of it, and my mind will catch up eventually. I will just keep thinking on these things and will not stop being amazed that I have found this kind of favor in God's sight. I won't stop being amazed until I die.'* To further help Mary believe all of this, the angel is telling her that her cousin, Elisabeth, has also conceived in her old age, and that **"nothing is impossible with God."** I wonder when Mary began to ponder how to explain to Joseph that she was pregnant by the Holy Ghost, when she began to ponder how to explain *this* to all of her family. God arranges for her cousin to be visited with pregnancy also, a special child to her, a forerunner of Jesus Christ, who will point to His coming and be able to prophecy that "one is coming who will baptize you with fire of the Holy Ghost." Oh, that we would receive God's Word to us as quickly as Mary receives it and believes it and never backs up from it. Oh, that we would just ponder on some of the Words the Lord speaks to us for a while instead of broadcasting them to others who cannot receive and believe. Oh, that we would **wait believing** until everything He has spoken to us comes to pass.

> When Mary visits Elisabeth, Elisabeth proclaims: **"Blessed art thou among women, and blessed is the fruit of thy womb. And whence is this to me, that the mother of my Lord should come to me? For lo, as soon as the voice of thy salutation sounded in mine ears, the babe leaped in my womb for joy. And blessed is she that believed: for there shall be a performance of those things which were told her from the Lord." (Luke 1:42-45)**

Elisabeth, the prophet's wife is **prophesying** that the child Mary is carrying is Her Lord. Mary has a confirmation and a witness, something more to "ponder." Do you ever wonder what the reaction of Mary's parents was to this news? Did God confirm in them this miracle, or did she receive rejection from them? Scripture says she spends three months with Elisabeth. Is that because her parents reject her, her family rejects her, and only Elisabeth receives a witness revelation from the Lord that the child Mary is carrying is the Holy One? There is a lot not said in the Bible about what Mary may have gone through to be blessed. The Bible does say that Joseph finding out she was with child set about to put her "away privily." He was going to break the engagement before the angel appeared to him also and told him not to be afraid to marry her. Did she spend three months with Elisabeth being rejected by Joseph **before** the angel spoke to him to go ahead and marry her? I can assure you that Mary went through persecution, just as Jesus went through persecution. We deceive ourselves if we think we can live for Jesus as the Bible instructs, obey His Word, and avoid persecution. The dark things of this world do not appreciate His light shining through you.

Joseph does marry her, and Mary has the baby in a stable. Shepherds appear next, saying that an angel has appeared to them, proclaiming, **"Fear not: for, behold, I bring you good tidings of great joy, which shall be to all people. For unto you is born this day in the city of David a Saviour, which is Christ the Lord. And this shall be a sign unto you; Ye shall find the babe wrapped in swaddling clothes, lying in a manger.** Then the shepherds witness a multitude of the heavenly host praising God, and saying **"Glory to God in the Highest, and on earth peace, good will toward men." (Luke 2:10-17)** They expound all of this to Mary. It is in verse 19 we see Mary keeping the words and pondering them in her heart. After her purification, she and Joseph go to sacrifice at the temple. At that point, Simeon prophesies over Jesus.

> "For mine eyes have seen thy salvation, Which thou hast prepared before the face of all people; a light to lighten the Gentiles, and the glory of thy people Israel." (Luke 2:30-32)

> "And Joseph and his mother marveled at those things which were spoken of him." Mary has more to keep in her heart and ponder. Simeon speaks again to Mary, "… Behold, this child is set for the fall and rising again of many in Israel; and for a sign which shall be spoken against; (Yea, a sword shall pierce through thy own soul also), that the thoughts of many hearts may be revealed."(Luke 2:34-35)

Mary is pondering this, also, I am sure. Then Anna follows up, prophesying and thanking the Lord, and speaking of Jesus to all them that looked for "redemption in Jerusalem." I am sure that Mary pondered this too, keeping it in her heart right up to the day she saw her child crucified, the meaning becoming all too clear. The day of the crucifixion, not only was Jesus pierced through, but Mary's own soul was pierced through as she viewed His torment and ultimate betrayal.

Following the account of Simeon and Anna prophesying over Jesus as a baby, our next account is of a twelve year old Jesus. Joseph and Mary go to Jerusalem after the feast of the Passover, and when they leave, Jesus stays in the temple, learning about His Father. Mary and Joseph look for him three days before they find him, and Mary begins to scold him for the stress he has caused them. He answers, **"How is it that ye sought me? Wist ye not that I must be about my Father's business?' (Luke 2:49)** When you start staying after the things of God, giving time to study His Word and spend time in prayer and at His house, you are going to upset some people around you, too. It is not going to be convenient for all of your loved ones that you are selling yourself out to the things of God, and that is your first focus. Can you pay the price of being about your father's business? **Luke 2:51** says, **"And he went down with them, and came to Nazareth, and was subject unto them: but *his mother kept all these sayings in her heart."*** She is pondering again. How could anyone absorb how great a thing the Lord had blessed to this young woman?

I am sure she studied and marveled after this son all of the time. As Jesus was growing, how many times did she go over the angel appearing to her, Elisabeth's prophecy, Simeon's prophecy, Anna's prophecy, Jesus speaking about being about His father's business at the age of twelve? She understood that Jesus could take care of the wine situation at the wedding. She brought the problem to him. He seemed to be reluctant almost, and she tells the servants to do what he asks. He then performs his first miracle of turning the water into wine. I am sure she pondered this often.

Other things she must have pondered:
The great miracles her son began to perform
His trial before Pilate
His cruel and bloody beating
Every step he took to Golgotha
Every cruel blow as the soldiers nailed him to a cross
Every ragged breath as he fought for air, struggling
on the cross, this child she was blessed to
deliver, now a man delivered to a cruel cross, who
will bring deliverance not only to a lost
world, but even to her
His words to the man he would take to paradise with him
His crown of thorns
His humiliation of being stripped of his robe
The unsightly torment that was inhumane
The sword finally piercing his side

The prophecy that not a bone would be broken
Simeon's prophecy a sword would also pierce her soul
The gift of the tomb
His resurrection and every word he spoke the forty
days he walked again on earth with her and
his disciples
The ten days she waited after his ascension for the
sending of the Holy Ghost to carry her and
comfort her until she herself would get to go to heaven
Every word and act from his birth to his death
Mary, the mother of Jesus
Pondering about it all again and again and again.

We weren't blessed to be there and take it all in, were we? But we can ponder it all over and over again, can't we? And we do as Christians, don't we? Why and how could he suffer so much? The Word says He looked at the "joy beyond the cross." Mary had to understand and look for the joy beyond the cross too. To carry our cross for Jesus, we too will have to look beyond any persecution, suffering, trial, or test.

When the angel first appeared to Mary, she saw the great blessing, but I doubt she saw all of the cost. She couldn't have borne it if she could see everywhere from that day that the blessing would take her and the cost of having the blessing. There is a cost to bear for the blessings of having our Lord, isn't there? When we submit ourselves as Mary did, however, and say, "Be it unto your handmaiden as you will," there is coming a great blessing for our obedience that we cannot see at first. Sometimes, we can see just the cost, but the blessing is coming. The pain for this mother was intense, wasn't it? Mary said she was blessed among women. There was pain and cost mingled with the blessing, though, wasn't there? There isn't another woman who has had this kind of blessing, this kind of calling on her life.

I know there are many things that the Lord has spoken to me, and if you are reading this and have earnestly been living for the Lord for a while, that He has spoken to you. He has spoken promises to us that He will keep, instructions to do things that when we have obeyed, He has blessed us for the obedience. There have been some costs, some minor ones daily that go along with serving a God that not everyone knows or understands.

There have been some greater ones that have cost us maybe personal desires or ambitions, as we determine to follow His leading for our lives, rather than our own. It may help to realize how much it may have cost Mary to be blessed as the mother of our Lord, all of those things that we can only imagine she may have suffered because she loved him as a son and recognized Him as Lord. All of the costs as those who were for him at some point rejected him toward the end of his ministry. (You too may have to stand alone at times with no support when you listen to and follow the Master.) When our children hurt, we hurt. Mary felt every stripe He took on His back in the deepest parts of her soul, didn't she? Every ragged breath He took on the cross must have ripped through every fiber of her being, didn't it? Many of us are mothers. You know what I mean.

I remember having a discussion with my youngest son one time. It was concerning the young man who was beheaded during the war, and it was put on the Internet. I had written my thoughts on the computer in an essay about this and Matt had seen it. Matt asked how his family could possibly want to see that. I understood that as a mother, if something like that had happened to one of my sons, I would have to see it just to be there in those last moments, even though that picture would never leave my mind. I would owe him being there and enduring the pain in some measure, too. I understood it anyway. Mary and other women followed Jesus to the cross. Mary was there through the entire thing, seeing every moment of the tormenting pain, but seeing the love and care Jesus had for her even in His torment, as he gave his mother into the care of the disciple he loved, and left her a son to care for, too. How many times did she ponder his great love for her?

I, too, have pondered many things the Lord has spoken to me and that I have read in His Word. I have reverenced the times in His presence and been in awe looking to the world he made for us. Things that He has spoken to my spirit that I have obeyed, not even understanding why He asked, but later understanding as the purpose He would take me to began to unfold. I have observed others learning about God, young people often, not quite believing, but yet beginning to ponder the things of God. I know you understand what I am talking about. There are things you are pondering at this point in your walk with God. There are questions raised in your mind about where He is taking you next; what does He want of you? How soon is His coming? He isn't afraid of your questions. It isn't doubt to inquire of the Lord. He wants us to ask of Him; He wants us to inquire what He would have us do; He wants us to willingly offer ourselves, as Mary did, to be His handmaidens, serving Him and serving His church, serving the lost.

What did Jesus come for? Why did Jesus suffer? Why did Mary suffer? The suffering was so you and I could be blessed, so you and I could be saved. Any suffering that you and I endure as soldiers of the cross of Jesus is so others can be saved by the witness of our lives as we endure any persecutions, looking for the joy beyond this life, as Mary did, and as Jesus looked forward to the joy beyond the cross when He would claim souls unto His kingdom. What a mighty God we serve! Jesus is deity and to be worshipped. Mary is human, blessed **among** women, not **above** women, but oh, how blessed she was!

WEEK NINE WORKSHEETS

Don't Lose What He Speaks to Your Heart

"But Mary kept all these things, and pondered them
in her heart." Luke 2:19

Has the Lord spoken to you in these Bible studies?

____

____

Has He directed you to begin doing something?

____

____

If you have begun to pray specifically for things, what have you seen answered?

____

____

Do you still have fear of others' opinions about what God is calling you to do?

____

____

I have prayed for each person that reads these Bible studies and works to do what is in them, that the Lord will bless and anoint you to do exploits for Him. We are at that time!

List here everything that LOOKS impossible in your life.

____

____

Say aloud: "For with God nothing shall be impossible."

Say it again. Go ahead, say it again. Be it unto you as you have spoken and as God has spoken. When we speak His words, we are finally getting "successful Christianity" right.

Mary had a lot to ponder, didn't she? Do you know what I think? I don't think she went about broadcasting what the angel told her. I don't think she raised Jesus, going around her village, pointing to Him and acting haughty and proud of her position as the mother of the Son of God. I think that is why God chose her. She was humble. She was pure. She was strong in character. You and I may have been a long way from any of those things when we came to the Lord, but as we study His Word and let it renew us, as we get filled with the Holy Ghost and stay renewed with His Spirit, He can make us like Mary. We can even be refashioned to be just like Him. We can be humble and will need to be if we want to be used by God. He resists the proud, remember? We can be pure through the blood of Jesus and the washing of His Word. We can have strength of character by letting the Holy Ghost direct us and live in us, and by purposing in our hearts to do those things each day that build character, showing ourselves to be faithful before God and others. If we purify ourselves, and line ourselves up to be like Jesus, others will want to be like us and be drawn to Him. We bring ourselves into obedience, and when we do, He makes us like Him. Ponder that! Oh, by the way, you do know what "ponder" means, don't you? It means to "really think about something, to meditate on it."

We are supposed to meditate on the Word, aren't we?

"And blessed is she that believed: for there shall be a performance of those things which were told her from the Lord." (Luke 1:45) I find the end of this scripture interesting. What if Mary hadn't believed? I don't know, but I know that this scripture conveys she is blessed, she believed, and the performance of all that was said would occur. Some scriptures are soooo rich! This is one of the many. I see this several times throughout the Word. Blessings when we believe and obey, then we can expect to receive the performance of the promises of the Lord. How great is that?

This scripture is part of Elisabeth's prophecy to Mary shortly after the angel's visitation. Don't you know Mary has probably had to wrestle some with the angel's visitation before Elisabeth gives this prophecy confirming that the performance of the things which the Lord told her would come to pass would be performed? Maybe not, but I know I would have appreciated some more confirmations at this point; you know, the point where you aren't at church in the middle of His Spirit, but you are out in the world with all of the doubters and accusers. I like the confirmations that help establish the initial leading and speaking of the Lord to my heart. Don't you? What happens, though, when we know the Lord has spoken to us to do things, and not only is the world being negative, but our family is trying to put a damper on us, our brothers and sisters in the Lord are trying to hold us back? What are you going to do when this happens? I will tell you right now that if you are going to walk with God, you are going to have to fight for His blessings; every time the storms blow against you, and the doubters and mockers are raging, you need to push through and go forward; don't back up from anything the Lord has told you He is going to do through you. He can't use weak vessels; He will allow the test to come to see if you are strong enough and ready to do the work He is calling you to do. Strengthen yourself in the Lord through study of His Word and prayer. Daily!

What do you need to believe the Lord for today?

____

____

____

____

"Behold, this child is set for the fall and rising again of many in Israel; and for a sign which shall be spoken against; (Yea, a sword shall pierce through thy own soul also,) that the thoughts of many hearts may be revealed.)" (Luke 2:34-35)

Jesus suffered a great cost to save our souls. Mary suffered a great cost when she agreed to raise this precious son. If you take up your cross (really, not playing) you will suffer great cost at times in serving Jesus completely as He is trying to call you to do. Remember in our lesson on "The Baptism of the Holy Ghost" that we learned that one of the meanings of the word "tarry" is "to sit and count the cost"? Jesus had to endure the cross even though he was looking to the joy beyond the cross. We will have to endure persecution when we (really) take up our crosses for the Lord.

Count the cost here: Evaluate what ambitions, pleasures, or sins you may need to abandon now.

____

____

Write down everything that you have been pondering: Write down every question you have for the Lord about Him, His Word, his plans for your life, what small steps you need to take today to get to your future purpose. Everything you can think of that you want to know right now. Then, realize that He hears you: He has an answer: It will come in His time.

____

____

List your dreams here: Then ask God if it is His Will for your life? Give Him your dreams. See what He gives back to you. Be willing to exchange your dreams for your life for His dreams for your life.

____

____

Every time we are facing a circumstance, a mountain, or an order from God that seems overwhelming in our minds, we need to remember how big God is, that it is His kingdom, and it is His work, and we need to memorize Luke 1:37 and quote it to our own minds when we need to take control of our minds negativity and fear. For truly, nothing is impossible with God.

This Week's Challenges

Spend time DAILY in the Word and in prayer.

Do not be controlled by fear or people's words or actions.

Hear God's voice and obey and follow His direction.

Worship and praise Him daily.

Continue recording in your prayer journals--prayers and answers.

Memory Verses

"For with God nothing shall be impossible." Luke 1:37

"And blessed is she that believed: for there shall be a performance of those things which were told her from the Lord." Luke 1:45

WEEK TEN

Recovering and Waiting on Promises

All through the Word of God we see God speaking to men and women promises. We see them receiving those promises in a variety of ways: disbelieving at first, denying that it can happen to them or that they can be used, asking how it can happen, some quickly agreeing to obey and receive the promise, and some who even laugh when God tells them of their promise. Abraham laughed at one point with delight, but Sarah must have sort of snorted in disbelief; you know that laugh. Sarah, the wife of Abraham, the one who would have the son of promise: Isaac. Sarah illustrates some of the mistakes we, too, may make on our way to becoming women of faith. Her laugh is one of doubt when she hears of God's promise, but when the promise is fulfilled, it is turned to a laugh of joy. From doubt, Sarah next makes a mistake of impatience but finally learns how to get faith right as she learns to wait on the promises of God and discovers that "nothing is too hard for God."

This is the kind of faith we all must grow in to: the kind of faith where we know NOTHING is too hard for our God.

Pray this aloud: Father, your ways are so far above our ways. Help me to remember that every time I am tempted to act in impatience with a decision for my life that has not been sanctioned by you. You hold my destiny; you know the purpose you designed for me when I was yet in my mother's womb. Help me to live up to your Word and your Will and give me direction

for that purpose, Lord. Help me to be patient with your directions, promises, and timing so I don't mess up the great things you have planned for me and those around me. Help me to sharpen myself as an instrument you may use through study of your Word for cleansing and instruction, and through prayer times with you that I may receive your power for doing the work you have set before me. I am exclusively yours. In Jesus Name. Amen.

Woman of Faith
Sarah
Mother of Nations

Before we get to Sarah, we need to look at the promise coming to Abraham first. Those of you who are married have found out that God may speak to you and to your husband separately about things, in this way confirming His Word to you. He spoke to Abraham first.

> "After these things the word of the LORD came unto Abram in a vision, saying, Fear not, Abram: I am thy shield, and thy exceeding great reward. And Abram said, Lord God, what wilt thou give me, seeing I go childless, and the steward of my house is this Eliezer of Damascus? And Abram said, Behold, to me thou hast given no seed; and, lo, one born in my house is mine heir. And, behold, the word of the Lord came unto him, saying, This shall not be thine heir; out of thine own bowels shall be thine heir. And he brought him forth abroad, and said, Look now toward heaven, and tell the stars, if thou be able to number them: and he said unto him, So shall thy seed be. And he believed in the Lord; and he counted it to him for righteousness." (Genesis 15:1-6)

The new covenant is even beginning in the Old Testament through Abraham. Just as he is counted righteous for his faith in God, those of us who are baptized into Christ Jesus become righteous through our faith in Jesus Christ.

The Lord goes on in this chapter to make a covenant with Abram concerning giving the land to his seed. I am sure Abram shares all of this with his wife, Sarai, but Sarai decides God is not going to use her in her old age to provide this child to her husband, so she helps God out. You know, God wants us to help him as he instructs us to help him. He doesn't want us jumping out ahead, or deciding that we need to do His part for Him. God performs the miracles, God gives the promises, God speaks to our hearts about what He is going to do through us. We are not the one's doing the performing; we are the one's making our bodies available for His use, in His time, to perform and do His will. You will notice from this next passage that when Sarah decides to take things in her own hands it brings a series of problems.

> "Now Sarai Abram's wife bare him no children: and she had an handmaid, an Egyptian, whose name was Hagar, And Sarai said unto Abram, Behold now, the Lord hath restrained me from bearing: I pray thee, go in unto my maid; it may be that I may obtain children by her. And Abram hearkened to the voice of Sarai. And Sarai Abram's wife took Hagar her maid the Egyptian, after Abram had dwelt ten years in the land of Canaan, and gave her to her husband Abram to be his wife." And he went in unto Hagar, and she conceived: and when she saw that she had conceived, her mistress was despised in her eyes. And Sarai said unto Abram, My wrong be upon thee: I have given my maid into thy bosom; and when she saw that she had conceived, I was despised in her eyes: the Lord judge between me and thee." (Genesis 16:1-5)

It would seem that Sarai is blaming Abram here for what she has asked him to do. The mistake here is impatience. God has promised and Abram has believed, but Sarai looks at the circumstances of her advanced age and decides without inquiring of the Lord that Abram should take Hagar to make the promise come about. Let us consider how costly this not inquiring of the Lord is. Sarai has brought another woman into her husband's life, a woman who now thinks she is better than Sarai because she has conceived Abram's child. (Another lesson on getting lifted up when we get promoted is in there somewhere. Later!) Now, there is strife in the house and Sarai wants Abram to fix the problem. The Lord eventually tells Abram to send Ishmael and Hagar away as Sarai has asked. Strife may leave the house, but don't you know that Abram misses this son that he believes he is not going to get to see anymore. It causes heartache when we choose without asking God first. God can remove our sins, but not all of those consequences of our sins. Nations that came from Ishmael are still fighting the nation that came out of Isaac today. Brother against brother, because both wanted to be the son of promise, but only Isaac was the promised son. That is quite a price for not asking God first how He wants it done; quite a price for impatience.

Sarai almost gave her position in God's covenant to Abram to someone else, didn't she? God meant for Sarai to be the mother of the promised child, but she almost gives her part of that promise to Hagar, and Hagar is lifted up because she believes she is the mother of the promise. She has had a child for Abram, not Sarai, so she feels that she is somehow elevated above her mistress, Sarai. When we try to usurp authority, we get everything out of order, don't we? Sarai is not waiting on God's time; she tries to make the promise happen, and she brings grief to herself, to Abram, and to Hagar, who is brought very low. God is so merciful to go ahead with His plan, but the promise to make nations from Abram's seed must be fulfilled also, and God promised nations to Ishmael as well as Isaac. Abram agrees to send Hagar away now with a son he loves, Ishmael, as the Lord commands him to do. I would feel sorry for Abram, but he did not ask God if that was how the child should come either, before he took Hagar to wife. He did not have to give in to Sarah when she suggested going in unto Hagar for a child.

In chapter 17 of Genesis, we see recorded the Lord appearing to Abram again when he is 99 years old, establishing again the covenant He will make with Abram's seed, telling him nations and kings will come out of him, renaming him Abraham, and renaming Sarai, Sarah. In chapter 18, the Lord appears again to Abraham, in what we refer to as a "theophany" of the Lord. The Lord appears in many ways through the Old Testament, doesn't He? Three men have appeared to Abraham and he recognizes it is the Lord.

> "And Abraham hastened into the tent unto Sarah, and said, make ready quickly three measures of fine meal, knead it, and make cakes upon the hearth. And Abraham ran unto the herd, and fetched a calf tender and good, and gave it unto a young man; and he hasted to dress it.

And he took butter, and milk, and the calf which he had dressed, and set it before them; and he stood by them under the tree, and they did eat. And they said unto him, Where is Sarah thy wife: And he said, Behold, in the tent. And he said, I will certainly return unto thee according to the time of life; and, lo, Sarah thy wife shall have a son. And Sarah heard it in the tent door, which was behind them. Now Abraham and Sarah were old and well stricken in age; and it ceased to be with Sarah after the manner of women. Therefore Sarah laughed with herself, saying, After I am waxed old shall I have pleasure, my lord being old also? And the Lord said unto Abraham, Wherefore did Sarah laugh, saying, Shall I of a surety bear a child, which am old? Is anything too hard for the Lord? At the time appointed I will return unto thee, according to the time of life, and Sarah shall have a son. Then Sarah denied, saying, I laughed not; for she was afraid. And he said, Nay; but thou didst laugh. (Genesis 18:6-15)

Between chapter 18 and 21, the dividing of land with Lot happens, Sodom and Gomorrah happens, and Abraham even lets Abimelec, king of Gerar, take his wife, Sarah, into his harem; fearing for his own life, he claims only part of the truth, that Sarah is his sister, rather than his wife. Fortunately, the Lord interferes before Abimelec lays with Sarah, or we would have the promise being messed up again, by Abraham this time. (Just a side note here: God must have been rejuvenating Sarah greatly to get her ready to conceive a child, because this is a very aged Sarah that the Bible says "was fair to look upon" and she is taken into a king's harem??? Maybe we just need a little more of His Spirit in us!)

"And the Lord visited Sarah as he had said, and the Lord did unto Sarah as he had spoken. For Sarah conceived, and bare Abraham a son in his old age, at the set time of which God had spoken to him. And Abraham called the name of his son that was born unto him, whom Sarah bare to him, Isaac. And Abraham circumcised his son Isaac being eight days old, as God had commanded him. And Abraham was an hundred years old, when his son Isaac was born unto him. And Sarah said, God hath made me to laugh, so that all that

hear will laugh with me. And she said, Who would have said unto Abraham, that Sarah should have given children suck? For I have born him a son in his old age." (Genesis 21:1-7)

God spoke a son of promise to Abraham. Sarah tried to make it happen through Hagar. God comes again and speaks the promise; Sarah laughs and then denies she laughed to God because she is afraid. Abraham also almost messes up giving Sarah to Abimelec, but God intervenes again to make the promised seed come through not only Abraham, but Sarah. God's greatest promises will never come through our works of the flesh. He does not want to share His glory with anyone. If He promises us something, we obey and wait, and He fulfills His promises. That is how we get the promise of the Holy Ghost, too. We believe without doubting, we obey God, and we wait until we get it.

Two things we can learn from Sarah, as well as Abraham, are not to be impatient of the promises of God. We are told to tarry for the promise of God, waiting before Him. Sarah delayed the promise out of impatience and Abraham almost delayed the promise out of fear for his life, but the Lord intervened, and Sarah was kept clean unto her husband. If we are going to be women of faith for our God, we are going to need to learn to hear His voice more and more; we are going to have to learn to wait on Him for the things He has promised us, and we are going to have to let faith prevail in our walk with God, rather than fear.

Our God has appeared in various ways and spoken various things to men and women. He has a time and place and divine purpose for what He wishes to be accomplished through men and women. He has a divine purpose for each of us in His kingdom and the promoting of it, if we will answer the call to labor for Him. Our God has presented Himself as creator, redeemer, comforter, among many other precious attributes, which are all summed up through Jesus Christ, the only name of God given by which we can be saved.

We do not understand all mysteries of God; we have had some revealed to us as He has revealed who He is in Jesus Christ. I am thankful that Abraham and Sarah did believe, that we are able to obtain the same righteousness that Abraham and Sarah obtained through faith. I am so glad that Sarah got hold of faith, that God was patient with her, as He is with us, even when we are being impatient with Him concerning His promises for our lives. I am so thankful that He doesn't write us off as soon as we almost mess everything up, but patiently lines us back out. Thank God for His promises and be faithful to wait and keep believing Him.

"Is anything too hard for the LORD?..." Genesis 18:14

Let us purpose to stay in the Word, to stay before the Lord, to wait on His promises, to obey immediately every call He makes to us, to become doers of the Word, and to obtain His promises through abiding obediently with Him in prayer to get our direction.

When we get our direction from the Lord and begin to walk into our purpose, we may have to wait. Actually, just plan on it: you are going to have to wait. For one thing, you aren't ready, and only God will know when you are ready, following how well you make it through the trials and tests that will come. Do you know how many years it was between God promising Abraham that he would have a child and become the father of many nations? It was 25 years. Do you know how long it was between when God spoke to Moses that he would deliver the children of Israel until he was sent to do it? It was 40 years. Do you know how long it was from the time David was anointed to be king of Israel until he took the throne? It was 13 years. Do you know how long it was before Joseph became second in Potiphar's house? It was 13 years that his trial of slavery and imprisonment lasted, plus however many years before that trial began that he had the dream of his family bowing to him.

Once God speaks His purpose for your life to you, hold on to it; hold on to it through the trials and the tests that will come. Strengthen yourself in discipline as a good soldier of the cross while you wait. When you stay obedient to God and make sure you have prepared yourself diligently for your purpose, the time will come for the fulfillment of the promise, and you will be so glad you waited patiently, because the timing of the Lord is perfect. Remember, when it gets hard, trust Him more.

The following is an excerpt from John Wesley's diary. I crack up every time I read it, but then I usually sober up, because I know that at this point I do not have the perseverance this man demonstrated--a perseverance that all of us must establish in our walk with God or we will keep falling short of the promise by quitting on the Lord too soon.

Sunday a.m., May 5, preached in St. Ann's, was asked not to come back anymore.

Sunday p.m., May 5, preached at St. John's, deacons said, "Get out and stay out."

Sunday a.m., May 12, preached at St. Jude's, can't go back there either.

Sunday p.m., May 12, preached at St. George's, kicked out again.

Sunday a.m., May 19, preached at St. somebody else's, deacons called special meeting and said I couldn't return.

Sunday p.m., May 19, preached on the street, kicked off the street.

Sunday a.m., May 26, preached in a meadow, chased out of meadow as a bull was turned loose during the services.

Sunday a.m., June 2, preached out at the edge of town, kicked off the highway.

Sunday p.m., June 2, afternoon service, preached in a pasture, 10,000 people came to hear.

God called John Wesley to preach, and I have never studied his sermons, but evidently he wasn't "tickling their ears." He was getting tossed out and intimidated everywhere he went. God put it in 10,000 people's hearts to go hear him preach AFTER THE TEST. We may feel like no one wants the message as we look around at the hardened hearts in our society today, but God is placing a hunger for Him within hearts today. When He has servants **prepared** to feed them, they will come. It is our job to prepare ourselves for the work He has called us to, and it is our job to help prepare hearts by sowing seed. How will they hear unless someone is sent?

> "When He has servants prepared to feed the hungry, servants who have sanctified themselves for service, then they will come, and the Lord will do wonders among us."

WEEK TEN WORKSHEETS

Recovering and Waiting on Promises

In Genesis 15:1-6 a principle of our righteousness being established through faith is first introduced as God counts Abraham's faith for righteousness. Many nations will come out of Abraham's seed and because Jesus made it so, we as Gentiles are able to be grafted in to the promise and adopted as sons and daughters when we believe in Jesus Christ, receiving the promise of salvation through our faith in him.

Do you understand that we are made sons and daughters in this same promise because of our faith in Jesus Christ?

____

____

Why did we get grafted in?

____

____

Consider how strong your faith is at this point in your walk with God. Abraham was in his 70s when God first told him he would have a son. Sarah was right up there with him, I am sure, for the Word says, "It had ceased to be with her as with women," meaning she was beyond the menopausal years. If you were in your 70s, even knowing the story of Abraham and Sarah, and God appeared to you and told you he would be sending a son of promise to you, would you receive that immediately and wait for God to perform that promise?

____

____

We can't be too hard on Sarah, can we? This is an example to us, though, that whatever the Lord is asking us to do, or whatever He has spoken He is going to use us to do, we need to believe Him to perform it.

Are you having patience with God and His promises to you?

____

____

What are you doing to prepare yourself to be used by God?

____

____

If you have been rocking along 10, 15, 20 years just studying His Word at home, worshipping Sundays and Wednesdays at church, praying only when you have needs, and now God is calling you to do a specific work in the body of Christ, how are you planning to further equip yourself for the work?

____

____

Lesson one: God promises and instructs, we obey, God performs.

Lesson two: Don't give away or hinder His promises to you through impatience or trying to help God do the performing of the miracle.

Lesson three: Grow in the Lord and learn to wait, and wait in faith through all the trials between the promise and the performance.

Lesson four: Laugh with joy at His promises, not with doubt.

Lesson five: Nothing is ever too hard for God.

Sarah waits through the dividing of the land with Lot; she waits through the period of Sodom and Gomorrah, she waits though Abraham giving her unto Abimelec. God enjoys delighting us, so laughing with joy and gladness is always appropriate, just no snorts of disbelief. Okay?

I know that many Christians are trying to survive by going to church and hearing a sermon on Sunday, maybe making it to Wednesday night service. If they are a carnal Christian, they may be spending their time in pleasure after work the rest of the week. Maybe they have never developed the discipline of Bible reading, a prayer closet time daily with the Lord. Maybe they do not listen to teaching on tapes, read Christian literature, or listen to godly music during the week. If this is where you are, and you are beginning to desire to move more into the things of God, you must develop a disciplined and consecrated time daily with the Lord, and you must evaluate your lifestyle and make changes if you wish to please God, get more in His presence, and be used to bring others into His marvelous light.

This Week's Challenge

Read 3 chapters a day in your Bible.
(You will read it through in a year)

Establish time in the morning to seek God's direction for your day.

Establish time after your workday to study your Bible and pray for needs.

Create a prayer place in your home with a Bible, notebook, prayer journal, pen, note cards, devotion book, concordance, Bible dictionary, teaching tapes, Christian literature and Bible studies, CD player and CDs of Christian music. (It is important to create a special place that is for God and you alone--you don't fold clothes there--you don't cook there--you don't talk on the phone there--you don't look at the computer there--just you and God.

Memory Verse

"Is anything too hard for the Lord...?" Genesis 18:14

WEEK ELEVEN

When Ye Fast

"When you take food out of the picture for a few days, you have time to think of God, to inquire of Him, to get direction, and to subdue your flesh and mind."

I did not want to fail to address fasting in this Bible study, not because I am a great practitioner of it, but because I know it is a powerful accessory to prayer that the Lord meant for us to practice to gain strength and power and to stay on top of our flesh. (I know how excited some of you may be that we are finally to this lesson.) I do believe when we understand all of the benefits for our spiritual lives, however, we will truly be more excited about incorporating fasting in our lives. This Bible study has been about overcoming hindrances to our faith, stirring up the spiritual gifts in us to help others in the faith, and staying full of the Holy Ghost to increase our faith and power for our ministry. If we are doing these things, when we add fasting and prayer to these, it will be like adding NOS to a race car. NOS is that extra burst of power right at the end of the car race that the driver incorporates to put his/her car through the finish line first. The Lord wants us to stay supercharged, too, for the race set before us. Fasting is that super charge that the Lord has instructed us to do not only to keep a handle on our flesh, but to increase power in our lives when mixed with prayer. A praying and fasting church will grow, because when sinners bound by sin come through the doors, they are needing deliverance and they will receive that in a strong praying and fasting church. So, whether you are regular and devoted to fasting at this point, whether you have never fasted in your life, or whether you have a medical condition that you feel prevents you from fasting, I want to present some things on fasting that should encourage you to incorporate it in your walk with the Lord as He directs in His Word and guides you individually by His Spirit.

> **Pray this aloud: Father, I wish to do your will for my life. I recognize I have been self-absorbed most of my life, and there are so many selfish ways yet in my nature. I acknowledge that I know and do very little about true sacrifice for those around me. I want to be used, Lord, to minister to those around me who need your salvation, but also recognize that you wish for me to be meeting carnal needs of food, clothing, and shelter as I am able. I recognize I am called to pray and fast to keep myself unspotted from the evils in this world, and to keep my focus on serving others rather than myself. I recognize that I need the extra power that fasting and prayer bring to my Christian walk. Help me to be moderate in a nation that seemingly has no concept of the word. Help me to keep under my flesh and to allow Your Spirit to control my desires that they are pure and for a good purpose. I wish to always be a lady and an ambassador of Christ and His church. Help me not to fail you and the lost you place in my path. In Jesus lovely name. Amen.**

> "Moreover when ye fast, be not, as the hypocrites, of a sad countenance; for they disfigure their faces, that they may appear unto men to fast. Verily, I say unto you, they have their reward. (Matthew 6:16)

I wished to use this scripture in Matthew first because I believe there are many Christians who have never fasted, and have no idea that it is something they should be doing. Note that Matthew 6 says, "when ye fast," not "if ye fast." God wants us to do it a certain way also, if we want the right and needed benefit from the fast. He wants us to look as we do on any other day, not announcing to the world that we are fasting. We want to make sure we obey this so we obtain the Lord's reward and not the world's. We may agree to fast together at times, so we would know we were fasting, but the world doesn't have to be told. Keep it between us and the Lord.

Sometimes we have a favorite verse in the Bible. I have a favorite chapter in the Bible. It is Isaiah Chapter 58. I feel that it is so full of promises, promises that we may obtain when we obey the LORD. Some of God's greatest blessings are promised to us in Isaiah 58 when we learn to fast the way the Lord desires us to fast.

> "Is not this the fast that I have chosen, to loose the bands of wickedness, to undo the heavy burdens, and to let the oppressed go free, and that ye break every yoke? Is it not to deal thy bread to the hungry, and that thou bring the poor that are cast out to thy house? When thou seest the naked, that thou cover him; and that thou hide not thyself from thine own flesh?" (Isaiah 58:6-7)

Let's break God's purpose for our fasting down just a moment.

No. 1--**to loose the bands of wickedness**--if we need some deliverance in our lives, or if someone else needs deliverance from not only sins, but even from weights, or those things that hinder us in our walk, we can break it with fasting.

No. 2--**to undo the heavy burdens**--there are going to be things that come into our lives, heavy trials, that can immobilize us walking with the Lord if we are weak Christians, but through fasting and trusting God we can remain strong through the trial.

No. 3--**to let the oppressed go free**--we have people all around us bound by drugs, alcohol, and every immoral thing imaginable. It is our duty to fast and pray for the deliverance of our neighbors and family from the bonds of the oppression of Satan.

No. 4--**that ye break every yoke**--We belong to Jesus now and Satan should not have any part of us. If we have any area still in bondage to him, something we have let slip back in and get hold of us, the quickest way to break that yoke is through fasting and prayer.

The second part of what the LORD wants a fast to do after we get deliverance from everything, is that we can now get out of ourselves and our selfishness, and begin to do those things that he has desired us to do, the things that make us real Christians, because they are the things that when we do them, it is exactly like doing them for Jesus personally: feed the hungry, clothe the naked, shelter the homeless, and care for and keep relationship with our families. Do you know what the Bible calls "pure religion and undefiled"?

"Pure religion and undefiled before God and the Father is this: to visit the fatherless and widows in their affliction, and to keep himself unspotted from the world." (James 1:27) Unfortunately today, a lot of what the Christian world is doing in the name of religion is still man's tradition and not pleasing to God. Fasting can help us purify ourselves, get the mind of Christ, and it can help us focus on what is important to God, help us to strengthen our relationship with Him, help us to stop being selfish, and help us to lay our lives down for God and others.

> "Then shall the King say unto them on his right hand, Come, ye blessed of my Father, inherit the kingdom prepared for you from the foundation of the world: for I was an hungered, and ye gave me meat: I was thirsty, and ye gave me drink: I was a stranger, and ye took me in: Naked, and ye clothed me: I was sick, and ye visited me: I was in prison, and ye came unto me. Then shall the righteous answer him, saying, Lord, when saw we thee an hungered, and fed thee? Or thirsty, and gave thee drink? When saw we thee a stranger, and took thee in? or naked, and clothed thee? Or when saw we thee sick, or in prison, and came unto thee? And the King shall answer and say unto them, Verily I say unto you, Inasmuch as ye have done it unto one of the least of these my brethren, ye have done it unto me. Then shall he say also unto them on the left hand, Depart from me, ye cursed, into everlasting fire, prepared for the devil and his angels:" (Matthew 25:34-41)

At the end of this chapter concerning judgment day, it is stated that those who did not do these things would **"…go into everlasting punishment: but the righteous into life eternal.(Matthew 25:34-45)**

We might say that fasting is not only to help God become strong in us so that we have power to help deliver others and break every yoke, but we can see from these scriptures that fasting is to help us get our priorities straight about what we are supposed to be doing for the Lord. That is everything that we do to meet the needs of those around us as those needs are presented to us; it is like we are doing that to the Lord, and we are going to be judged on whether we did or did not do.

When you take food out of the picture for a few days, you have time to think of God, to inquire of Him, to get direction. We spend a lot of time shopping for food, preparing food, and eating food. When we deprive ourselves of food, our body becomes weak, but that is when God can become stronger in us. This is much to be desired if we want to grow closer to God and hear from Him and receive overcoming power.

Our strongest witness is when we are meeting needs and doing all we can to provide for those needs. Probably one of the reasons why America is still so blessed even though we have great wickedness in our land, is that our government still uses our taxes to take care of the needy, and still rewards in the tax system those who give benevolently, not only favoring those of us who tithe and make offerings to church, but honoring every contribution to help others.

> "As we have therefore opportunity, let us do good unto all men, especially unto them who are of the household of faith." (Galatians 6:10)

When we see brothers and sisters in the faith, not just our local church body, but all sisters and brothers in the faith, and see a need in their life, and we have the means to assist them, and fail to do so, we are missing it. We are living in a very selfish world today where everyone is all about me, but God has brought us out of that into "His marvelous light," and we want to be great examples of meeting needs. We won't have trouble keeping people coming to church if we are loving them and caring about their needs as much as our own. I think we know and understand that this is the will of God. I think this helps explain why we fast, and before we go on to specifically how we fast, let us just take a moment to look at one more thing in Isaiah, and that is an example of how the Hebrew people were fasting at that time, and how God does not want us to fast.

"Wherefore have we fasted, say they, and thou seest not? Wherefore have we afflicted our soul, and thou takest no knowledge? Behold, in the day of your fast ye find pleasure, and exact all your labours. Behold, ye fast for strife and debate, and to smite with the fist of wickedness: ye shall not fast as ye do this day, to make your voice to be heard on high. Is it such a fast that I have chosen: A day for a man to afflict his soul? Is it to bow down his head as a bulrush, and to spread sackcloth and ashes under him? Wilt thou call this a fast, and an acceptable day to the LORD?"(Isaiah 58:3-5)

Our day or days of fasting are not to find pleasure for ourselves, so we shouldn't be lying in front of the television or going shopping or reading a book for pleasure. I know that when I fast, it brings a call to more order in my life and I am seeing things I want to do and take care of around the house, paperwork to file, the checking account to balance, a closet to clean out. Because you have more time from not cooking and eating, you are tempted to "exact all your labours" to take your mind off not eating, but this is not what the Lord wants us to do on those days. He wants us to get before Him, to draw nigh to Him, to pray for those who need deliverance, to ask Him to cleanse us from impurity in us and around us, to prepare us to have more power in praying for those who need deliverance, and to prepare us and empower us for our specific ministry. If you are going to fast (and the Lord wants you to do so), you need to do it right. You need to prepare before you launch into a fast, so your body gives you the least amount of trouble. If you eat sugar or drink caffeine drinks, that can give you a problem on a fast. I have had unnecessary headaches and ended up throwing up through most of my fast because I failed to eliminate all of these things several days before going on my fast. You want to be able to have the benefit of being able to focus on God. Besides obeying God, receiving more power in our prayer life, and eliminating selfishness and other strongholds, there are health benefits of fasting. They include clearer skin, sloughing impurities out of your body, helping to get a handle on overeating, and helping to discipline you more and more as Jesus' disciples. If the Lord has called you out to do a work for Him, you need to give even more time to fasting and prayer, to receive direction, to subdue the flesh, and to strengthen your spirit against the onslaught of temptations the enemy is going to bring when he sees that you are about to be used in a new area of service.

What was the first thing Jesus did when he began his ministry, as soon as he was baptized? The Spirit drove him to the wilderness where he began a 40 day fast. Well, we always say a 40 day fast, anyway; actually, I believe Satan began to tempt him after 40 days to eat when he became hungry. He did not give in, so it must have gone longer than 40 days. Jesus was both man and God. As God, he understood the power he would need as a man to conquer the flesh before the temptations came to the flesh he had limited himself to. When Satan does come to tempt him, he is ready. His flesh he is in doesn't want to go hungry anymore than our flesh would want to go hungry. Satan offers him part of what he has come for, but the cost would be failure and leaving Satan still dominating the earth. He had fed his spirit for 40 days, rather than his flesh, he knew the Word, and he had determined his obedience to it. He conquered the flesh and Satan.

There is a point where Jesus is asked why he and his disciples do not fast. He does not brag to them that he has fasted more than they ever thought about fasting. He simply answers in **Mark 2:20: "But the days will come, when the bridegroom will be taken away from them, and then shall they fast in those days."** Again, if we think fasting is not a necessary ingredient in our Christian lives, we may want to note that Jesus says, **"Then shall they fast in those days."** (after he is ascended). He intended for us to fast to stay strong. He intended for us to fast to have increased power to minister. When the disciples could not cast out a demon, He admonished them for unbelief, but then he told them "some things can only come out by prayer and fasting."

I wanted us to look at types of fasts from a biblical perspective so we can identify how we may best incorporate and use fasting. There are possibly nine different types of fasts observed in the Bible, but I just want to speak of what is practical for us to begin to actually institute fasting in our Christian walk as a regular discipline. None of us would want to tackle anything close to a 40 day fast unless led by God, and then He would supernaturally provide for us. The ultimate fast for us should be a complete fast which includes no food or water. If we need a breakthrough in our life, we need to help in deliverance to those around us, or we need to get a grip on some weight or sin trying to resurrect and get hold of us, this is where we need to go. To do this fast without getting such a severe headache you can't pray, you need to go off sugar and caffeine gradually a few days before you begin. Try to schedule this fast when you do not have to be working so many hours in a day that you can't give time to prayer and quietness. Spend extra time in prayer. Pray specifically for deliverance needs and revival. This would be effective if several in a church would do it together, also. If you have never fasted before, just commit to one day. When you see that you are handling it all right, you may wish to extend it for three days.

Allow me to share one of my first little fast stories. It sounds laughable, but when we are a new Christian, God honors so quickly all of our efforts because our hearts are so in love with Him. I was teaching a four-year-old Sunday school class with another young sister in the Lord. We had two little boys who did not have a mother in their home, so we were a little partial to them. We found out the oldest boy had received a diagnosis of something that could be fatal, and we both became adamant that nothing was going to happen to that little boy. We agreed to fast lunch together the next day and pray. (Lunch! That was our big sacrifice with prayer to intercede for this little boy). The next time we went to church the little boy had an "all clear" report from the doctor. The world would say right here that the doctor got it wrong the first time. Women of faith know that God is mighty and hears and answers prayer. I have fasted a "little" more seriously than this since that time.

If you have never fasted before, begin with a one day fast the way the Jewish people do it. I would still go off sugar and caffeine a few days before. The day before your fast, eat a normal evening meal around 5 to 6 P.M. Do not take any water or food from that time until a normal meal the next day between 5 to 6 P.M. Every time you are thinking of food, you need to go to prayer and open your Bible and study. This fast is to get hold of your flesh, to help someone pray for a need, and to get in agreement to break through for a specific need. If you are trying to go deeper with the Lord, you could do this two times a week just for the discipline, not to announce to everyone that you are doing it as the Pharisees would have done.

If you have a medical condition such as blood sugar problems and need to eat regularly, truly examine your present diet and see what you can eliminate for a few days, such as sugar, (which is probably aggravating most health problems) or really eat a minimum every time you need to eat. I believe that God will honor anything you do to restrict your flesh, which is what a disciple of Christ should be practicing. We are instructed to be moderate in the Word of God and we all know that Americans as a group are far from being moderate in food because we are so blessed with so much of it. Just because we are affluent enough to buy all the food we want does not mean that we should eat all we want. We can become moderate and gain the benefits of a disciplined diet and please the Lord with our discipline. I remember going to Weight Watchers when I was first in church, and I told my mother-in-law that I felt more spiritual just staying on that diet. She was the one who pointed out to me the scripture about avoiding "surfeiting." She said I was being more spiritual because I was avoiding surfeiting. I did not even know what that word meant. (It means overindulgence in food and drink.) Most of us do this daily and laugh about it, but the Lord tells us to avoid this and to be moderate before others. If you want to make yourself more accountable to eating healthier, and at this time due to a blood sugar problem, diabetes, or other health disorder, you cannot go without food all day, I have incorporated a record keeper in your worksheet that you can carry to help you follow a healthy pyramid of eating. Print copies to carry with you. It should benefit you not only in eating healthier, but also in avoiding surfeiting, and should help you to drop any excess weight on your body slowly, but surely, if followed.

There are different types of fasts listed in the Bible; I was researching and I think around nine different fasts are there. You are probably familiar with the Daniel fast in the Bible that you may wish to study out that is mostly vegetarian. Just don't start teaching vegetarianism, because the Lord has made it clear that meat is fine for us to eat as long as we cover it with prayer. There are times when it may not be viable for you to go completely without food and water for medical reasons, so this fast may be a way for you to incorporate fasting.

When I first got in church, I fasted "somewhat," every now and then. I never committed to do anything on a regular disciplined basis. The most I ever fasted was four days. I know we have people in our congregation who have gone on fasts as long as 10 days without water, so I know the Lord supernaturally sustained them to allow them to do that. I did drink water on my four day fast; I just did not take in any food. I very much felt that the Lord called me recently to begin to fast more, so I have tried to incorporate it more, but I am aware that He wants me to go further. I believe He wants all of us to go further.

Fasting and prayer cause you to be God conscious. Fasting also can speed up healing.

> "Then shall thy light break forth as the morning, and thine health shall spring forth speedily: and thy righteousness shall go before thee; the glory of the Lord shall by thy reward." (Isaiah 58:9)

Is this not what we want? These are such rich promises and why I love this chapter in the Bible so much. To have the glory of the Lord shining forth in us and to be rewarded with an upsurge of good health is a great and needed benefit of doing the fasting the way the Lord wishes for us to do it. If we need another big "why" to do the fasting, this passage of scripture should really be motivating. There is more to the fasting God wants us to do than to help bring salvation and deliverance. He wants us to feed and clothe the needy, and bring the homeless to our houses, and make sure we are caring for our families. He wants us to keep our spirits right. What does he say he will do when we get the fast right? We will be casting off darkness and hindrances, we will increase healing to our bodies, our righteousness will be more apparent, and the glory of the Lord will be our reward. We are going to get more in the Lord's presence when we fast and pray.

Woman of Faith
Esther

> "For if thou altogether holdest thy peace at this time, then shall there enlargement and deliverance arise to the Jews from another place; but thou and thy father's house shall be destroyed: and who knoweth whether thou art come to the kingdom for such a time as this?" (Esther 4:14)

"…who knoweth whether thou art come to the kingdom for such a time as this?"

Every once in a while the Lord will drop a phrase from His Word into my spirit. Several years ago, He dropped the phrase "for a time such as this" into my spirit. I think about all of the Word I have read, all of the sermons and Bible studies and teaching tapes I have listened to, all of the studying of His Word, and I know that all of that has been put into me and you for a reason, and that reason is not just to keep us saved, but it is to prepare us for service to minister. I believe you and I are at a pivotal time like Esther, a time where we can do and be a part of the deliverance work the Lord is bringing about, or we can allow it to come through others. I want to be used by the Lord and be a part of the work; I don't want my call and part to pass to someone else. I don't think you do either.

Most of us will be familiar with the story of Esther. When King Ahasuerus' queen, Vashti, refused to come before the King, it caused a proclamation to go forth in the kingdom that "wives are to obey their husbands." Vashti is to be replaced, so ten virgins are brought to the kingdom to go through a purification process to try and be selected by the king. Esther, an orphan, has been raised by her uncle Mordecai as his daughter. She does not make it known that she is a Jew. She goes through a year of purification and readies herself and finds favor not only with the king, but with the man overseeing the selection process. The king selects her, and a man by the name of Haman in the king's service, offended by Mordecai's not bowing to him, asks for a proclamation to go forth to get rid of the Jews. The king does not know that Esther is a Jew. Mordecai tells Esther that perhaps she has come to the kingdom for such a time as this. He suggests this may be Esther's destiny. I believe we have been prepared, and the Lord is calling us to sanctify ourselves for the glorious things He is about to do. We don't want to miss our destiny because we aren't ready and sanctified. Esther sends word to Mordecai to have the people fast food and water for three days that the king might agree to see her. She is granted that favor and wisdom on how to approach the king, and ends up with the terrible things planned against the Jews happening instead to the man who has planned it and his sons.

If we want favor with our king, we might wish to emulate Esther in the following ways:

1-- Prepare ourselves for kingdom work by study of His Word and prayer.

2-- Make ourselves as presentable as possible as His bride and ambassadors.

3-- Purify our hearts, minds, bodies through renewing our minds in His Word and fasting.

4-- Approach God with the reverence and awe He deserves.

5-- Ask for guidance and walk in His wisdom.

WEEK ELEVEN WORKSHEETS

When Ye Fast
Correct Attitude of Fasting

"Moreover when ye fast, be not, as the hypocrites, of a sad countenance; for they disfigure their faces, that they may appear unto men to fast. Verily, I say unto you, they have their reward. (Matthew 6:16)

Should we smile and look energetic when we are fasting?

____

____

Should we tell everyone that we are fasting so they will appreciate how spiritual we are?

____

____

Whose reward do we want?

____

____

Things Accomplished by Fasting

"Is not this the fast that I have chosen, to loose the bands of wickedness, to undo the heavy burdens, and to let the oppressed go free, and that ye break every yoke? Is it not to deal thy bread to the hungry, and that thou bring the poor that are cast out to thy house? When thou seest the naked, that thou cover him; and that thou hide not thyself from thine own flesh?" (Isaiah 58:6-7)

Who do you know that is bound by wickedness, by drugs? Write their name down here:

____

____

What burden are you carrying that you need to give to God? Write that down here:

____

____

Who do you know that is being oppressed by a tyrant husband, by selfish grown children, etc.? Write their name here:

____

____

Do you have anyone in your church who is poor, needy, in shabby clothing?

Write their name here:

____

____

Now, pray for the first three and consider whether you have extra money, food you can sacrifice, or clothing that the last group can use. See that you get it to them today.

Do you have family that you are avoiding or neglecting to help care for?

See them today or call them today. Isaiah 58: 6-7 is God's first purpose for a fast: to break wickedness. His second purpose is to prepare us to minister to others: feed, shelter, clothe, and care for your own household. In essence, to get our minds off of us and superficial wants and take care of real needs in our world; in so doing, we are doing unto the Lord.

> **"Pure religion and undefiled before God and the Father is this, to visit the fatherless and widows in their affliction, and to keep himself unspotted from the world."(James 1:27)**

Fasting prepares us to do the ministry the saints are called to do. Remember that before Jesus began His ministry He went on an extended fast to prepare Himself. If He needed to do that, I am sure that we need to, if we wish to be effective in ministry. At one point, when the disciples fail to cast out a demon, after Jesus deals with their unbelief, he then states that, "some things only come out through prayer and fasting." So, if we are not getting breakthroughs in our spiritual growth, in helping others get delivered, in seeing revival come to our church, we definitely need to be adding fasting to our prayers, and increasing both.

> Fasting will help us get hold of our flesh, but prayer is our connection to the source of our strength and power.

Guide for Fasting

1. When God requires you to fast, obey Him for how long to fast.

2. Schedule regular fasts to add discipline to your walk and to get breakthroughs.

3. Go off caffeine and sugar gradually a few days before your fast.

4. Abstain from all food and water for a complete fast.

5. Spend time in specific prayer--you should be fasting for a specific purpose.

6. You may abstain from food only and sip some water throughout the day.

7. To do a one day fast, eat at 5 or 6 P.M. one night and go until 5 or 6 P.M. the next night without eating or drinking for a one day fast. You can do this one twice a week and do it while working. Just remember to find times to pray at lunch and extra time in the morning and at night.

8. If it is really a struggle for you to fast because of blood sugar problems, eat several times a day, but eat extremely moderately to take part in church fasts.

Promises in Isaiah 58 to those who are fasting for the right reasons:

You will reflect more of God
Your health will increase rapidly

**Your righteousness will be apparent
We will have more of the Spirit of God in our lives**

Woman of Faith
Esther

**"For if thou altogether holdest thy peace at this time,
then shall there enlargement and deliverance arise to
the Jews from another place; but thou and thy father's
house shall be destroyed: and who knoweth whether
thou art come to the kingdom for such a time as this?"
(Esther 4:14)**

She is God's kind of woman, isn't she? She is knowledgeable of God's ways, she is prepared and trained for the kingdom; her loveliness is more than skin deep, so she finds favor with the one over the virgins as well as the king; she purifies herself before she goes before the king; she knows strength and favor come through prayer and fasting. She cares about others.

Is it God's job or ours to control our flesh?

____

____

Think of three ways that you can keep on top of things that try to control your flesh:

____

____

This Week's Challenge

**Read and study the book of Esther this week.
Fast one day and pray for revival in our communities.
Use your pyramid chart to study and change
to healthier eating patterns.
Make changes to become fit vessels for our King.**

**Continue reading three chapters in the Word a
day to read the Bible through in a year.
Use your prayer journal often to see your answered prayers.**

Memory Verse

**"Pure religion and undefiled before God and the
Father is this, To visit the fatherless and widows in
their affliction, and to keep himself unspotted from
the world." James 1:27**

Copy the following guide and make extra copies to help discipline yourself with healthy moderate eating that gives you proper nutrients and fiber for your body. The chart is helpful to mark off your selections, to make sure you are choosing healthy, rather than junk, food for your body while you are reducing your weight. Eating moderately even when you are not fasting will help you stay focused and committed to disciplining your body. Commit to the following to learn to be moderate and to become healthier if you are overweight or feel sluggish from poor eating choices.

Checklist for Pyramid of Healthy Eating Choices

**Water 8-8 oz. glasses a day. For every 25 pounds
you carry over 200 pounds, add a glass.**

_____ _____ _____ _____ _____ _____

Milk (skim milk, yogurt, cheeses, ice cream 300 calories)

_____ _____ _____

Fruit (120-180 cal.)

_____ _____ _____

**Vegetables (up to 6 servings green type, not
beans, peas, or corn or potatoes)**

_____ _____ _____ _____ _____

Protein (lean beef, fish, chicken, peanut butter, eggs 300-500 cal.)

_____ _____ _____ _____

**Breads/Grains (wheat, pasta, beans, peas,
potatoes, oatmeal, rice 500 cal.)**

_____ _____ _____ _____

Oils/Dressings (200 calories)

_____ _____

Two 100 calorie snacks

_____ _____

To lose two pounds a week, if you are moderately active, you should be able to take your weight x 10 to equal number of calories to maintain your present weight. (Example: 200 lbs. x 10 = 2000 calories to maintain.) To drop weight, reduce by 300 calories a day. Increase movement.

*This page may be reproduced

WEEK TWELVE

Pray Without Ceasing

"Pray without Ceasing." I Thessalonians 5:17

Pray this aloud: Father, most of the world calling themselves Christian today still either are not praying enough, are not understanding the importance of prayer or what to pray for, or even following the examples of prayer you set forth in your Word. I want to be a woman who lights my world, a woman who knows how to get before you and travail for the lost, a woman who knows how to please you by offering thanksgiving, praise, and worship to you BEFORE I begin to petition you for needs. Help me to understand how much darkness and heaviness is lifted away through praise alone, and help me to incorporate more praise and thanksgiving to you when I come before you in prayer, continually letting praise be in my mouth. Help me to set aside time to sit with you in my prayer closet, allowing you time to speak to me, too, instead of pleading my petitions and racing off to my day. Help me to understand from Your Word how to pray without ceasing, how to pray and petition for things that will please you and advance Your kingdom, rather than seeking those things to consume on my flesh. Help me to have Your mind when I pray, and teach me how to go into deeper dimensions of intercessory prayer, to allow the Holy Ghost to pray through me with groanings I cannot understand. Help me to reach

new places in prayer that go beyond my understanding and take me into the Spirit as I give myself to allowing the Spirit to pray through me. I desire to be your handmaiden and vessel for Your Spirit to minister to this hurting world that those in this world might come to the saving knowledge of Jesus Christ. Amen

This final lesson is on prayer. If you have taken care of your hindrances, are seeking God to fill you with His Spirit, and are open and giving yourself to the Lord to use you as He wills in the gifts of the Spirit, you are aligning yourself with the Word of God, and when you begin to add specific prayers for specific needs, spending time going before God for others, and you add fasting to those prayers, you will become a prayer warrior for the Lord. You will be a real force in breaking down strongholds and seeing captives of darkness set free into His marvelous light. Every time you bow before the Lord and go to prayer with Him, you are saying, "I know you are God; I know you have all the answers; I know that I cannot do anything unless I abide in You and allow You to abide in me." If you will begin to consecrate more time to prayer, not only will you be going into His presence more often, not only will you be breaking strongholds for others, but you will begin to get a clearer focus and more power for your ministry in the body of Christ. Fasting will help us get hold of our flesh, but prayer is our connection to the source of our strength and power. We must know how and for what purpose we are praying. In this lesson we will look at why we need to pray, what we need to pray, and how we need to pray.

> "And it came to pass, that, as he was praying in a certain place, when he ceased, one of his disciples said unto him, Lord, teach us to pray, as John also taught his disciples."
> (Luke 11:1)

How?

Jesus responded with the "Lord's Prayer." You have probably had several studies on this if you have lived as a Christian any time at all. It cannot be bypassed, however. We need to realize how important this is. The disciple that asked Jesus this was already praying, but he could see that things were happening when Jesus prayed, so he wanted to know the SECRET. The Lord answered him. We teach this prayer to children in Sunday school, and it is such a great prayer said verbatim just as it is stated in scripture, but if we learn and memorize this prayer, it is also a model for HOW we should pray when we go before the Lord.

> "And he said unto them, When ye pray, say, "Our Father which art in heaven, Hallowed be thy name. Thy kingdom come, Thy will be done, as in heaven, so in earth. Give us day by day our daily bread. And forgive us our sins; for we also forgive every one that is indebted to us. And lead us not into temptation; but deliver us from evil. (Luke 11:24)

It is stated a little differently in Matthew, but the same pattern. We must approach the Lord in the following ways if we want our prayers to meet God's requirements to hear and answer us.

1. Acknowledge Him as Father and as Holy.

2. Pray for our obedience to His Will as in heaven.

3. Supply our spiritual and physical needs.

4. Forgive us.

5. As we forgive everyone.

6. Keep us from temptation and evil.

If you find it difficult to focus when you go to prayer, say the "Lord's Prayer" verbatim before you begin to be thankful. If you are still losing focus, try singing to the Lord, then begin to thank Him for everything you can remember that He has ever done for you. At this point, I have never had trouble getting into prayer, because He inhabits the praise of His people, and when His Spirit shows up, your flesh quiets down. This is the best example from scripture on HOW to pray because it came straight from God's mouth. The "Lord's Prayer" is a form example of how to approach the Lord in set-aside time for prayer. We may and should be talking to the Lord throughout the day. I thank Him through my day. As soon as I see someone with a need, I say, "Help them, Lord, comfort them, strengthen them, and intercede for them." We do not have to go through form all day, is what I am saying, but there should be daily prayer closet time where we are communicating with God and gaining strength and power from being in His presence. If we have that committed time each day, we have power the rest of the day to just speak His name and request as needed, and He then shows up readily because "we are **abiding in Him** and **have Him abiding in us."**

We are also commanded to pray in the spirit, as well as the understanding. **"…I will pray with the spirit, and I will pray with the understanding also:…" (I Corinthians 14:15)**

Ask the Lord to help you pray in the Spirit. Pray for everything you know with your understanding and then spend time just praising and magnifying Him, staying before Him, and as you feel impressed to pray for someone or some need, truly give yourself to that, and you will begin to pray in the Spirit. You will grow in this area with time given to it. We are a McDonald's world, and we want it NOW, but God is not going to snap to for some of our instant gratification needs. He wants you to spend **time** with Him. He wants you to give that **time** to Him.

Who?

Who do we pray for? Let me direct us to some scriptures that are particularly important for our world today, and for our prosperity and peace.

> "<u>Pray for the peace of Jerusalem</u>: they shall prosper that love thee." (Psalm 122:6)

> "But I say unto you, Love your enemies, bless them that curse you, do good to them that hate you, and <u>pray for them which despitefully use you</u>, and persecute you; (Matthew 5:44)

> "And when he had thus spoken, he kneeled down, and <u>prayed with them all</u>. (Acts 20:36--Paul praying with other disciples)

Other scriptures instruct us to <u>pray for those in authority over us </u>that we may live peaceful lives; any other thing we see in the Word that is <u>God's Will for us</u>, such as the <u>salvation of souls, deliverance of people from captivity, our families</u>; we are instructed to <u>pray for ourselves that we do not enter into temptation;</u> we are instructed to <u>pray for one another (other disciples).</u>

What?

"Likewise the Spirit also helpeth our infirmities: for we know not what we should pray for as we ought; but the Spirit itself maketh intercession for us with groanings which cannot be uttered. And he that searcheth the hearts knoweth what is the mind of the Spirit, because he maketh intercession for the saints according to the will of God." (Romans 8: 26-27)

The things we can see and know in the natural--the needs for us and others-- we can pray with the understanding for those things, but we cannot see in the spirit, and we need to be able to pray in the spirit, so that God can pray through us for those things He knows the needs that we cannot know with our natural minds, needs that need to be interceded for in the saints' lives and in the sinner's lives. (I have listed the things I pray for at the end of this lesson, and set up a prayer checklist for you to create for your prayer time each day with the Lord).

Why?

It pleases God; it is how we communicate with Him; it is how He communicates with us. **Revelation 5:8 says, "And when he had taken the book, and the four beasts and four and twenty elders fell down before the Lamb, having every one of them harps, and golden vials full of odours, which are the prayers of saints."** In the Old Testament, animals were sacrificed on the altar and burned. This was what God required for a pleasing sacrifice. In this dispensation of grace, our sacrifice is praise and as we see in this scripture, our prayers (the prayers of saints) are odours kept in golden vials. In another place in scripture, it says that these prayers of saints come up for a memorial before Him. When we pray, He hears and He answers. He does not forget. There is a time and a place that is right. Daniel prayed and it seemed to be 21 days before the answer came, but scripture recorded that the answer was on the way immediately, but some angelic battles took place between the sending and receiving.

As soon as we see a need, as soon as we arouse an attack from the enemy, as soon as God places a person in front of us that is unsaved, we should see it as our duty as a good soldier of God to go to prayer. Just as soon as we recognize the need, because if we say in our minds we will pray about it later, we may very well forget. If you see someone in your workplace that is ill, that is depressed, pray for them then. When someone asks us to pray for them, we need to stop responding, "I will be sure and pray for you." If you forget, you just lied. Take their hand and pray for them right then. They just asked you to do so. God is not limited to space and time, remember, so if someone calls and asks you to pray with them about something, say, "Let's pray together right now on the phone." God is not offended, and you will not forget after chatting with them to do what you said you would do. We pray because God "answers" when we allow Him to abide in us, and we continue to abide in Him in prayer and study of His Word. He tells us to ASK.

"Watch and pray that ye enter not into temptation: the spirit indeed is willing, but the flesh is weak." (Matthew 26:41) If we do not stay prayed up, our flesh will take over and lead us in wrong paths. Prayer brings strength from God. We cannot do this Christian walk by the arm of the flesh, and we cannot stay on top of our flesh without praying for His strength. Besides watching for ourselves, we need to pray and watch for our sisters and brothers so they will not fall. Jesus set this example when He revealed to Peter He had prayed that his faith would not fail him.

> **"But I have prayed for thee, that thy faith fail not: and when thou art converted, strengthen they brethren."**
> **(Luke 22:32)**

Those of us who have been converted are to be strengthening our brethren through praying for them, too. If we are going to be strong Christians, we will not be racing around trying to get everyone to pray for us and our every little need; we will learn to pray for ourselves, and even when we are in our own heavy trials, we will still remember to pray and intercede for our brothers and sisters in the Lord.

> "Is any among you afflicted? Let him pray. Is any merry? Let him sing psalms. Is any sick among you? Let him call for the elders of the church; and let them pray over him, anointing him with oil in the name of the Lord: And the prayer of faith shall save the sick, and the Lord shall raise him up; and if he have committed sin, they shall be forgiven him. Confess your faults one to another, and pray one for another, that ye may be healed. The effectual fervent prayer of a righteous man availeth much." (James 5:13-16)

We pray if we are afflicted, we call for the elders of the church to pray if we are sick, that we may be healed. Prayer makes things happen. Many Christians today do not practice confessing faults to one another, but the above scripture tells us to do so and pray for one another, that we may be healed. We might want to begin to practice this, and we do want to be a trusted sister in our church that others can have confidence in when they confess their faults to us that all we are doing is praying for them, not gossiping about them.

"But I have prayed for thee, that thy faith fail not: and when thou art converted, strengthen thy brethren. (Luke 22:32) I have already said this, but we need to pray for our brothers and sisters in the Lord that their faith would not fail. When I have had some times of crisis during my Christian walk, I could feel the prayers for myself from my brothers and sisters. I was strengthened. I have tried to be faithful to pray for those who I recognize are struggling in their walk. God hears and helps. A few times I have felt too weak to pray, and have just sent up, "Jesus, have someone pray for me. Don't leave me." He must have used someone to help pray for me, because I regained strength.

> **"But the end of all things is at hand: be ye therefore
> sober, and watch unto prayer." (I Peter 4: 7)**

We are responsible to watch for our souls, our churches, our families. We are to take it seriously because the end is near. We want to be saved and we want to save as many as we possibly can. When we keep time consecrated to Him each day in prayer, we are abiding in Him, and He says He will abide in us, and we can ask whatever we will and have it done for us.

Is there a proper posture for prayer? Knees? Standing? Lying prostrate on the floor? I believe we should approach God with awe and reverence when we pray. Sometimes, I lie in bed and pray, and the Bible says to do so. Many times I pray on my knees or lay in the floor, because I feel a need to be in a "posture of submission" to Him. (I have recently felt led by the Lord that He does want us on our knees more in church). I stand praying in church with my hands lifted at times (not to be seen of men), but because my church practices this when we pray corporately aloud. Remember in our former lesson on gifts of the spirit we read in I Corinthians for "men to pray everywhere with lifted hands" and then women likewise. I often pray out loud, especially when praying in the spirit if I feel a strong unction to pray that way. Sometimes, I am very much praying fervently when I get focused and am praying back and forth in the understanding and with the Spirit. It is quiet, but fervent at times. It is intercession. Daniel prayed three times a day standing at a window. I sometimes rock back and forth when interceding. I pray the "Lord's Prayer" verbatim at times. I speak scriptures such as Psalm 23 as praise before I begin praying specifically at times. I speak to the Lord throughout my day as I need calmness and strength and wisdom. I pray the scripture when I am beginning to praise Him, and do speak familiar phrases of praise to His name. I do not wish to be repetitive or pray in vain, but I have searched the scriptures for how He likes to be addressed and use that. On a final note concerning prayer: Don't get bogged down with form, just talk to God and take all of your cares and concerns to Him. Do always remember to approach Him as you would a king that has all power, but a king who is your daddy, and I believe you will have the proper attitude posture to please Him. **Pray!**

Things I Pray

The peace and protection of Jerusalem
The protection of our churches and minister's families
The protection and salvation of our soldiers
The guidance of our president and protection of our nation
The provision, protection, sending of laborers
and souls to our missionaries
My families' salvation, protection, provision
My brothers and sisters in the Lord (specific needs to be filled
with Holy Ghost, healing, financial, gifts of spirit, their faith)
I pray the Jabez prayer often for my life,
my children's, and my church
"Bless me, indeed
Enlarge my territory to minister
Guide me with your hand
Keep me from evil
Help me not to cause pain or grief ever"
I pray for God to direct my steps in the morning, give me strength
and love for those I am around, give me divine appointments
to witness and wisdom in how to speak and conduct myself.
I pray for power, wisdom, and anointing for my ministry.

When we are told to pray without ceasing, we understand that we cannot pray every minute of every day, but we continually keep devotion and prayer times, we continually keep examining ourselves to keep our spirit right, asking God to search our hearts and correct us. We continually pray for revival in our land and churches. We pray for our needs and others. We never stop praying, because if we do, we start doubting. We need prayer to keep the **F.A.I.T.H.**

> We need prayer to keep the F.A.I.T.H.

Women who light the world and walk faithfully impact it for Christ. They are "doers" of the Word. They know what the Word says to do because they are faithful to study it every day, and they are faithful to assemble in a church under an anointed preacher and receive instruction, chastisement, and correct doctrine. These women (and I hope you have committed to become one of them) are passionate and sold out to the cause of Jesus Christ. Their talk reflects godliness everywhere they go; their dress reflects modesty; they make time to pray for souls; they make time to meet needs. These women do not have to make pronouncements to the world that they are Christians. The world knows who they are by their fruit.

Christian sister, a final note: Thank you for taking this discipleship journey with me. I have prayed that your **F.A.I.T.H.** would not fail.

Week Twelve Worksheets

Pray Without Ceasing

Take this review quiz first, and then we will incorporate any weaknesses into a prayer list.

From "Overcoming Fear and Negativity"

1. How do you overcome fear?

____

____

____

2. How do you overcome speaking negative things into your life and others?

____

____

____

3. What did the Shunammite woman say even when she could see that her son had died?

____

____

From "Overcoming Hurts Caused by Ourselves and Others"

4. What must we let go of to move forward in our walk with the Lord and to be able to minister to others and help them?

____

____

5. Do you remember the scripture that would be good to quote when Satan or others try to make us feel the above?

____

____

From "Overcoming Unforgiveness"

6. Who is the number one person we release for God's blessings when we forgive?

____

____

7. What else do we block from God when we don't forgive?

____

____

From "Overcoming Addictions"

8. Are you aware of any addictions you may have (physical or emotional)?

____

____

9. Are you working on overcoming them?

____

10. List your action plan to take hold of your flesh and dominate it:

____

____

From "The Baptism of the Holy Ghost"

11. Do you know how to teach a Bible study on this?

____

12. Are you staying refreshed and prayed through?

____

13. Do you have a regular prayer time daily to stay close to the Lord?

____

____

14. Are you inspecting your "fruit" before you put it out there for others to inspect?

____

____

From the Gifts of the Spirit Part 1

15. Are you developing your gifts and talents for the Lord?

____

16. In what ways?

____

____

17. Are you praying for the gift of "prophecy?"

____

____

From "The Gifts of the Spirit" Part 2

18. Whether you have the gift of mercy or service or not, we all should be compassionate and encouraging. In the past month, make a list of all those you have made a point to say an encouraging word to.

____

____

19. Now make a list of five people you want to encourage or do something specific and physical for.

____

____

From "Women's Roles in the Church"

20. Make a list of everything you believe you are able to do in the church you attend if asked or led to do.

____

____

From "Mary, Woman of Faith"

21. How quickly are you obeying God when you read something in His Word that you haven't been doing and should be doing?

---

22. When He speaks to you personally and challenges you to step out in faith, how quickly are you obeying?

---

23. What do you need to do to increase your faith and boldness?

---

24. Take a moment to reflect on what it cost Jesus to go to the cross for us, and also consider what it cost Mary to see her son mistreated and humiliated when she knew who He really was? If you have a line drawn mentally that Jesus has not been able to cross before, identify it and remove it so that you can be a vessel for His use.

From "Recovering and Waiting on Promises"

25. When God tells us what He is going to do in our lives, what should we do to prepare for the promises?

---

26. What two things should we not do?

From "When Ye Fast"

27. Why is fasting so important?

____

____

8. What should we do a few days before a fast to prepare for it?

____

____

From "Pray Without Ceasing"

29. List one reason we pray learned from lesson on each of the following:

Why?

____

____

How?

____

____

What?

____

____

Memorize the "Lord's Prayer" for a model for your daily prayers.
The Lord's Prayer (Matthew 6:9-13)

"Our Father which art in heaven, Hallowed be thy name.
Thy kingdom come, Thy will be done in earth, as it is in heaven.
Give us this day our daily bread.
And forgive us our debts, as we forgive our debtors.
And lead us not into temptation, but deliver us from evil: For
thine is the kingdom, and the power, and the glory forever.
Amen".

Create Your Prayer List and Model Here

First, write here how you will approach the Father (Acknowledge Him as God, pray His will, then speak words that glorify and praise Him)

____

____

Second, write your needs, your family's needs, your churches needs, your nations and communities needs (Any area not conquered in these lessons, record here and continue to pray for strength in those areas of your life).

____

____

Third, confess your sins and faults and struggles to the Lord. Ask for forgiveness, and release forgiveness to others.

____

____

Fourth, ask God to indwell you with His Spirit to help you overcome every temptation, and plead His protection as your shield against every attack of evil from the enemy

____

____

Fifth, spend time praising and thanking God, remembering all of the good gifts He has given you and all of the protection, provision, and the salvation, deliverance, and healings He has wrought in your life.

____

____

Sixth, sit quietly before the Lord with a pen and paper and ask Him to speak to you and direct you.

____

____

My Prayer for You, Christian Sister

Heavenly Father, Thank you for the hearts that are turned to you, the hearts that are seeking your face in prayer, seeking to know you more through study of Your Word, and seeking to know how they might minister to you and to your hurting world. I know that the ones who have read this book are hungry, and I know that you will continue to lead them to green pastures. I pray that you would protect their minds from those who are wolves in sheep's clothing. I pray that you would protect them and keep them from the hour of temptation that is upon this earth. I ask you, Father, to guard their hearts and minds, and to place them under anointed messengers who not only hear from you, but who are careful examples of your holiness before the world and their flocks. I ask that you would direct them through your Word how to overcome in every area where they need to subdue their own flesh and not be overcome by adverse circumstances. I pray for a bountiful measure of love, patience, and longsuffering to be given to these women, along with the wisdom and strength to work with and pursue those who need your salvation. Help their focus to be on you first, each morning, as their eyes open and their feet hit the floor, that they would turn their faces to the heavens and implore you for strength, guidance, and wisdom to reach the lost; and that they would implore you for grace to keep their own souls clean from this tainted world. Help them to fall in love more and more with a Holy God, and send supernatural strength to them to oppose the wearying that Satan is bringing against the saints of God. I ask that you would plant a seed of purpose in these women that is clearly defined in them, and that will grow to fruition as they purpose in their hearts to obey your instructions to them each day. Help them to remember that they must pull away from the daily demands and interruptions each day to spend times of refreshing with you if they wish the flow of your spirit to be continual, rather than blocked by cares of life overtaking them. I pray for my Christian sisters to be placed in churches of the Word, and that they will be used fully in the gifts that you have placed in them. Help them to always operate those gifts in love, to never be petty or jealous of others, but to be the saints that new converts can come to in confidence because they have proved themselves faithful. Help them to keep all of their armor on as they fight the good fight of faith, knowing that one day they will hear you say, "Well done, thou good and faithful servant." Keep us in your care, Lord. In the name of JESUS. Amen.

LaVergne, TN USA
20 September 2010
197704LV00003B/4/P